Doris Stokes is a celebrated clairaudient who has confounded sceptics with the uncanny accuracy of her readings. In Australia she filled the Sydney Opera House and was mobbed in the streets; in this country tickets are sold out for her demonstrations within hours; she has appeared on the Terry Wogan Show, and Desert Island Discs; had a TV documentary devoted to her; been presented to Princess Anne and receives hundreds of letters from her huge following every week. Her books, which tell how she discovered her extraordinary gift and how she shares it with the world, include VOICES IN MY EAR, MORE VOICES IN MY EAR, INNOCENT VOICES IN MY EAR and A HOST OF VOICES.

She lives in London with her husband John and their son Terry.

D0552490

Also by Doris Stokes

VOICES IN MY EAR: THE AUTOBIOGRAPHY OF A MEDIUM
MORE VOICES IN MY EAR
INNOCENT VOICES IN MY EAR
A HOST OF VOICES

DORIS STOKES
(with Linda Dearsley)

Whispering Voices

Futura

A Futura Book

ISBN 0 7088 2809 0

Typeset, printed and bound in Great Britain by
Hazell Watson & Viney Limited,
Member of the BPCC Group,
Aylesbury, Bucks

Futura Publications
A Division of
Macdonald & Co (Publishers) Ltd
Maxwell House
74 Worship Street
London EC2A 2EN
A BPCC plc Company

Chapter One

It was a hot summer day the first time I saw the house.

'Come and look at this Doris,' said Laurie and I walked up the road, puffing a bit because the heat was bouncing off the paving stones and making the air go swimmy and what I really longed for was a shady chair to rest my back and a long cool drink.

But then I saw it and for a moment the heat melted away.

Set back from the road and on a slope so you looked down at it, the house was blue and white with tiny lattice windows that glinted in the sun and a strip of garden ablaze with roses. There were matching blue gates folded neatly across the sloping drive and a pretty cottage-style front door.

'Oh it's gorgeous!' I cried in delight, and then with a pang I realized that a house as lovely as this would be far too expensive for me. 'Oh Laurie,' I said, suddenly disappointed, 'I wish I hadn't seen it. I could never afford that.'

But Laurie's not one to give up easily. He just shrugged and grinned his unstoppable grin. 'Well let's go and see shall we . . .'

It was a strange feeling, this house hunting for the first time at my age. In the past John and I had always been very grateful for whatever rented accommodation was offered to us. It might not look like something out of a glossy magazine but we filled it with our bits and pieces, put our pictures on the walls and made it home. Now, suddenly to be given a choice was a bit bewildering. And this business of walking into someone's home and wandering about inspecting the decoration — well I just couldn't get used to it. It always seemed so rude somehow to say no.

Yet it had to be done. It was the answer to a problem that had been worrying me for months. When John and I came to London we'd managed to get a flat in a block for disabled ex-servicemen because John is a disabled veteran of Arnhem. It wasn't a palace – in fact some people said the blocks were ugly – but it was comfortable and convenient and we soon had it looking cosy. We even made a miniature garden outside the front door with rows of plants in pots along the balcony and on summer evenings John and I could sit there in deck-chairs amongst our geraniums and busy-lizzies and pretend we were in the country.

In 1982 things got even better. As flats fell empty, the management began putting bathrooms into them. Until then we'd used a tin bath in the kitchen, but after a long wait, John, Terry and I were moved up the corridor to one of the converted flats. We paid a bit extra and had a shower installed as well and after a couple of weeks we couldn't imagine how we'd managed without it.

The improvement was so great that the blow that fell soon afterwards was doubly unexpected. The whole site was going to be completely redeveloped, the tenants were told. Our block was to be demolished to make room for a garden. The other blocks were to be modernized and in many cases two flats were going to be made into three.

We had a choice. We could live on a building site for the next five years while we waited for a flat in one of the other blocks to become available – though they couldn't guarantee we'd get another two bedroomed place – or we could find another home.

Now the spirit world has always told me not to worry – just to trust and we shall be provided for. But I couldn't help worrying. How could I do my sittings with the noise of building work going on all day? And how could we turn Terry out if at the end of five years we were only offered a one bedroom flat? The mobile home we'd bought as a country retreat might be a

6

solution, but it was tucked away in a quiet little backwater near Ashford in Kent. Lovely for holidays but it would be very awkward to carry on my work from there.

I lay awake at night wondering what on earth we were going to do, and all Ramanov my spirit guide would say was 'Trust, child.' Which was all very well for him but for me it was easier said than done.

John, who's not a worrier like me seemed to be just as unconcerned. 'Don't worry yourself love,' he used to say soothingly. 'It'll work out. You'll see.'

But I didn't see. The months went by and nothing seemed to happen except that I developed a very bad back. London became very hot and dusty the way it always does in summer and John and I were very glad when our holiday came round and we were able to go down to the van for some fresh air.

And then when I least expected it, the spirit world stepped in. It was an overcast day and my back was playing me up badly so when John said he thought he might go out for a bike ride I told him to go because all I felt like doing was sitting about with a hot water bottle. Yet no sooner had John pedalled away than I was bored. I'd finished my book the day before and I'd got nothing else to read. There was no one around to talk to and nothing on TV.

Dejectedly, I fiddled around with the remote control buttons. Terry had got us linked up to the Oracle and he was always looking at it, but I'd never used it. I wonder if I can get Russell Grant's stars? I thought. I always enjoy horoscopes. I pressed a few buttons and sheets of information began flashing across the screen but half of it was double dutch to me and there was nothing that resembled a horoscope.

Impatiently I pressed more buttons and then suddenly one of the bright pages caught my eye. It was nothing to do with Capricorn. It was a list of properties for sale at a London estate agents, and one of the houses in South London had three bedrooms and was surprisingly cheap.

I did a quick bit of mental arithmetic. If we sold the van and added our life savings I reckoned we could afford that house. It would be the answer to all our problems.

Excitedly I dialled Laurie's number. I don't think I've introduced you to Laurie. He's the latest addition to our team. To say he's my manager sounds rather grand and it's not really like that. In the last couple of years my work has snowballed so much that what with personal appearances, radio and TV, as well as my normal sittings, I couldn't cope with all the organizing. People kept saying you need a manager Doris but it sounded so official I dithered. Then one day I was introduced to Laurie O'Leary, and we hit it off straight away. Laurie had actually given up a management career for a more peaceful life but when he saw what a mess I was in he decided to go back to management to help me. So now Laurie looks after the bookings, sees to the travel arrangements and all the other bits and pieces that take up so much time. He's much more than a manager. He's like one of the family.

Anyway, on the phone that morning I told him I'd read about this house I thought I could afford.

'Okay, Doris,' he said, 'I'll come and fetch you tomorrow and take you to see it.'

Well John wasn't bothered. 'If it suits you, girl, it'll suit me,' he said. But he didn't want to interrupt his holiday to go trailing through a house. He'd much rather potter about with his roses in the garden at the van. And in truth I knew he'd feel like a spare part – after all women are much more interested in that sort of thing than men.

Instead, Nancy our good friend and neighbour from the flats, said she'd come with me. As it turned out that first house wasn't right. A young couple lived there and they'd worked very hard on it but it was too arty for me. There was a bare white room with one sofa

8

in it and flash shelves. They'd stripped down the doors to bare wood and built a big stone fireplace. It was beautifully done and would have been perfect for a young couple but not an old fashioned sort like me.

I wandered about making polite noises but Nancy, bless her heart, is a bit forthright.

'Well that'll have to come out for a start,' she said shaking her head at the fireplace. And, 'Oh no you don't like those doors do you, Doris? They'll have to be painted.'

It was obvious we'd have to spend a fortune on decorating to get it to our taste and I don't suppose the young couple were too pleased at the thought of us tearing out all their improvements. I think it was a relief all round when I explained it wasn't quite us.

The area was very nice however: convenient for the shops and central London but green and open with trees and flowers in every garden and the countryside an easy drive away. Laurie checked with another estate agent and this time we were in luck. The first house we were sent to was very nice but somehow it didn't feel right.

'We'll think about it,' I promised. My back was killing me by this time and I was quite prepared to go home again but that was when Laurie called me to look at the blue and white house he'd found.

I fell in love with it on the spot.

'Come on then, let's have a look inside,' he said ignoring my protests about the expense and the fact that we didn't have an appointment.

A tiny little lady opened the door and when she saw me her eyes flew wide in astonishment.

'Oh Doris Stokes!' she gasped. 'I never ever thought I'd meet you.'

Her name was Hilda and she led us round chattering brightly. The house was as lovely inside as out. There was a beautiful kitchen with work tops all round – no more trying to balance half-a-dozen plates on the kitchen table – there were patio doors looking out onto

9

the garden and a spacious bathroom. The bathroom was a bit of a problem though because it was downstairs.

'There's no way I'll get down stairs with my legs crossed first thing in the morning!' I said doubtfully.

'Don't worry about that, Doris, you could have a loo put in the bedroom,' said Laurie.

The other problem was that with my bad back I could hardly lift one foot from the ground let alone tackle those stairs. Never mind, said the others, they'd look at the bedrooms for me.

They clattered away and Hilda and I stood chatting in the hall. It was a particularly nice hall. Square and airy with a rich blue carpet and sunshine streaming in through the windows on either side of the front door.

'I do like this hall, and such a beautiful carpet.' I was saying, when out of the corner of my eye I saw a blur of movement. Someone else was heading up the stairs to the bedroom. It was a frail old man, taller than Hilda and rather stooped and by the way he hauled himself from step to step, pulling heavily on the handrail, I guessed he had difficulty walking. A flash of intuition told me that this was Hilda's husband and substantial as he looked – he was a spirit person.

'Excuse me, love,' I said suddenly to Hilda, 'but was your husband an invalid?'

'Well, yes he was,' she said in surprise.

'I thought so,' and I glanced back at the stairs. They were quite empty. The man had vanished. So I was right. He'd passed over but came back from time to time to visit his wife and his old home. Well that was alright by me. I've never minded sharing a place with spirit people as long as they don't make a nuisance of themselves.

There was a lot of clumping overhead and then the others, unmistakably of this world, came thudding down again.

'The bedrooms are lovely, Doris,' said Nancy, 'and

10

the one at the front looks right over that little green outside.'

But still I hesitated. I'd love the house. I didn't need to go upstairs to know I'd be happy here but I wasn't at all sure we could afford it.

Hilda must have read my mind. 'Look, Doris,' she said, 'I'd like to think you lived here. As it's you I'll bring the price down.'

'She'll take it!' said Laurie instantly.

On the way home of course the doubts set in. Oh dear what have I done? I kept thinking. Our life savings and I haven't even been up the stairs. I hope I'm doing the right thing. Our friends in the mobile home park thought we were mad. There they were selling their houses to move into mobile homes and here we were selling our mobile home to move into a house. At our age! But then John and I have always been impulsive. We married a week after we met and they all thought we were mad then. In fact I couldn't convince my family it wasn't a joke. When they discovered after the wedding that we were only too serious they shook their heads disapprovingly and said it wouldn't last. Yet here we are 40 years on, still going strong.

You know you're doing the right thing when everything goes smoothly, however, and soon it was obvious that the spirit world wanted us to have this house. The legal side went through without any bother and just when we were trying to decided on a moving date, another piece of good luck came along. I was talking to *Woman's Own* magazine on the phone one day and I told them I'd let them have my new address as soon as possible.

'I've got my house at last!' I said happily.

'Oh wonderful,' they said, 'you will let us design it for you, won't you?'

Design it for me? The idea of having a house designed had never crossed my mind, but the more I thought about it the more exciting it seemed. It was

11

true that Hilda's colour schemes wouldn't go very well with our furniture, but I haven't a clue about decorating. As long as a place is clean and comfortable I'm happy. But if someone else would sort out the paint charts and wallpaper . . . well, yes, it *would* be very nice to have everything matching and colour co-ordinated, as they say these days.

Well the house became legally ours by the end of the summer but we put off the moving date until December to allow time for the decorating to be done. In between we went down again with Deborah, nicknamed Dobs, from *Woman's Own*, to discuss the colours. Dobs had great plans. I couldn't quite picture what she meant half the time but she seemed to know what she was talking about so I thought it best to let her get on with it. At this point, though, I still hadn't been up the stairs and Dobs was very insistent that I should.

'Come on, Doris, you'll have to come upstairs,' she said. 'I must show you what I have in mind.'

My back was still twinging and I hadn't had any stairs for twelve years but it did seem ridiculous, so I held my breath and took a run at it. I flew up those stairs as if I was on a wire and when I got to the top I turned round and saw everyone was killing themselves laughing.

'You went up those stairs like a two-year-old!' giggled Dobs.

I couldn't help smiling. 'Yes well I didn't dare stop,' I confessed. 'If I'd run out of steam half way up I'd have been stuck.'

The planning stage didn't take very long because John and I were about to leave on the publicity tour for my book *A Host Of Voices*. We were going to be away three weeks and when we came back we were going straight into our new home. Terry was going to organize everything he said. He'd pack up all our things and arrange the whole move. I must admit I was a bit apprehensive. I was afraid I'd never be able

12

to find anything again, but Terry told me not to fuss. He was quite capable of managing.

Well John and I set off on the tour, but back at the house things were far from tranquil. The first we knew about it was when Steve, the electrician, refused to work in the place on his own. He wouldn't say much about it but we gathered he heard strange noises when no-one was there and his tools were always being moved about. He could never find them where he left them.

Laurie was the next one to realize something odd was happening. He and Steve left the house together one evening and before leaving they turned the lights off at the mains, as an additional safety measure. They banged the front door shut, went out to the car and as they glanced back they noticed that the light was on in the loft.

Bewildered, they went back and checked. But the electricity was still off at the mains. Puzzled, Laurie went up to the loft and switched off the light. Then they locked up again and went outside. By the time they reached the car, the loft light was twinkling brightly. Back they went, rather nervously by now and switched the light off once more, and this time they headed for the car at a near run.

'Come on, Steve, let's go for goodness sake,' said Laurie, 'or we'll be here all night.' And they sped away without looking back.

About an hour or so later Terry called at the house on his way home from work. Afterwards he phoned Laurie.

'Did you know you left the loft light on?' he asked.

Finally Terry discovered for himself what they meant. Arriving first at the house one morning, he went in, locked the door behind him and wandered into the living-room to see what the decorators had done. But as he stood there admiring the paint work, he heard the front door open again. Thinking it was Laurie he stuck his head into the hall to say hello but

13

to his surprise the hall was empty. The front door was wide open and no one was in sight.

Crossly Terry closed the door and was just walking into the kitchen when there came a great crash from upstairs. A portable light on a long cable had disengaged itself for no apparent reason and come smashing down onto the floorboards.

On later visits to the house with Laurie and Steve, the three of them were startled by further unexplained crashes and even the sound of footsteps crossing the boards above when everybody was downstairs.

In the end it became a joke. They christened their unseen visitor George and when he became particularly troublesome Terry would say, 'Oh pack it in George, or I'll turn the old woman on you!'

Funnily enough, since John and I moved in George has been quite peaceful. Occasionally a door will open silently and close again when there's no-one visible and we say, 'Hello, how are you.'

Recently I decided it was time we had a chat to get things straight, so I waited until the sitting room door opened all by itself and then I tackled George.

'Your missis doesn't live here any more,' I told him because I was certain it was Hilda's husband, and in case he was confused I explained where she'd gone. 'It's our house now,' I added gently.

He said his name wasn't George but Edward, nicknamed Ted, and the house used to belong to him. He couldn't understand why we were here stripping off his wallpaper and knocking things about. Once I'd explained he seemed quite happy.

'We don't mind you popping in whenever you like, Ted,' I said, 'but don't move things about. It makes life so difficult.'

And there have been no problems since. Ted wanders in from time to time but he doesn't bother us at all.

Not long ago we had another spirit visitor as well. I don't think we are particularly unusual in this. I think

14

that probably most houses are visited by previous occupants and people who were closely linked to the building, it's just that most people aren't aware of it, or dismiss strange noises and unexplained draughts as the wind, or the people next door.

Anyway on this particular occasion we'd had some bricklayers in building a garden wall and I put a strip of plastic down in the sitting-room to protect the carpet from their muddy boots. I was sitting there by the fire winding down before going to bed when I heard footsteps quite distinctly walking across the plastic. Everyone else was in bed and the sound definitely came from just a few inches away. What's more one foot came down much more heavily than the other so I knew this person walked with a stick or a pronounced limp.

'Who's that?' I asked.

'Reggie,' said a man's voice and then the steps faded away and he was gone.

Reggie? I thought. How odd. I was sure the man who used to live here said his name was Ted. So the following day when our next-door-neighbour Margaret came in, I asked her about it.

'Did the man who used to live here walk heavily on one side?'

'Oh no,' said Margaret, 'he was an invalid. You never saw him walk. He was either in a chair or in bed.'

'That's strange,' I said, 'I heard this man walk across my sitting-room and he came down very heavily on one foot so he must have had a limp or walked with a stick. He said his name was Reggie.'

To my amazement Margaret burst into tears. 'That's my husband,' she whispered dabbing at her eyes. 'You've just described my Reggie.'

So now we know that Margaret's husband has been in to have a look at us to check that we're the sort of people who'll be nice to his wife.

It certainly was marvellous to come back from our tour to a lovely new house. Terry had done very well

15

with the move and, though there are still one or two things I haven't found yet, practically everything was safely in one piece. Dobs had worked wonders and for weeks I kept wandering around reminding myself that this magnificent place really belonged to us and we wouldn't have to leave it soon and go home. It still seems a bit unreal.

Dobs' *'pièce de résistance'* was my bedroom which was done up like a beautiful birthday cake in pink and white with mirror doors on the wardrobes all along one wall to make it look twice as big. When she'd suggested the mirrors and all the other bits and pieces I hadn't the faintest idea what it would look like and I must say when I saw the end result I was staggered – in the nicest possible way!

I sat there in my pink chair with the frill round the bottom and looked at myself in the mirrors, all thirteen-and-a-half stone of me and I said, 'Sixty-five! You could have done with this girl when you were twenty-five! All these frilly pillows and scatter cushions and pink satin bows on the pictures, and all they've got to look at is Doris in bed with no teeth in and her indigestion pills!'

I was appearing on TV AM with Derek Jameson not long after this and I couldn't help telling Derek about my beautiful bedroom and the mirrors. Derek's an earthy straightforward man with a great sense of humour and I knew he'd enjoy the joke.

'Well you know, Doris, twenty-five years ago those mirrors would have done your sex life a bit of good,' he chucked, and of course I was in fits again.

A few weeks later on our wedding anniversary the delivery man came to the door with two packages. One was a single red rose in a long flat box with a card saying: Happy Anniversary, John and Doris, from Derek Jameson. The other was a square box which said: Happy Anniversary, John and Doris and the wardrobes. Also from Derek Jameson.

And the wardrobes? I said to myself. What did that

mean? Intrigued I tore off the wrapping paper. Inside was a crimson box with two black tassels on the top. What on earth could it be?

'D'you think it's an orchid?' I wondered aloud.

Laurie who'd just popped in suggested it might be stationery. John hadn't got a clue.

So I opened the box and inside was a black lace suspender belt, a pair of black silk stockings and a tiny wispy object that Laurie explained was a G string. The black tassels I'd thought were for opening the box were in fact to go on your boobs!

What a sight for the wardrobes that would have been, if only I'd been able to get them on!

Chapter Two

It was a very eventful summer that summer of '84 before we moved into our new house, and quite by chance we found ourselves caught up in a tragedy that moved the whole country.

The weather was very warm that year and so John and I, who're not well suited to the heat, tried to escape to our mobile home whenever we could. I was always glad when I could work from the van instead of our stuffy flat in London, and one particular week the van proved specially convenient because I was doing a demonstration at Tunbridge Wells – just up the road.

The show went well and afterwards I felt very drained, the way I always do, and I sat in my dressing-room drinking tea while the clamour of spirit voices faded away and the ordinary day to day world re-established itself in the the forefront of my mind. There were a lot of people milling about nibbling sandwiches but I didn't notice anyone in particular until Laurie came up.

'Doris, I'd like to introduce you to an old friend of mine, Ted Roffey.'

Ted was a slim, dapper man, he lived in the area and Laurie had sent him tickets for the show. He seemed to have enjoyed himself and he was very kind. He'd never seen anything like it, he said, fascinating. Certainly made you think. Then he steered a young a couple in my direction.

'They're dying to meet you, Doris,' he said. 'This is my nephew Tony and his wife Janet.'

They were a lovely couple. Very young, dark and a little shy and Janet of course was heavily pregnant. A pregnant woman is a wonderful sight I always think, so full of hope for the future, and yet when I looked at Janet it was as if a cloud passed quickly over the sun. There was a sudden coldness and I felt afraid for her for no reason I could put a name to. I looked at her carefully trying to work out what was wrong and noticed that she was wearing high heeled shoes.

'You want to get those shoes off, love, and put flatties on,' I said. 'You've only got to go over . . .'

Tony who was standing slightly behind, put his arms round her. 'I'll buy her some flatties tomorrow, Doris,' he promised and as he said it he leant forward and kissed the top of her head and there it was again. That quick pang of fear. There and gone again, before I could identify it.

'That's right. Give her all the love you can,' I said without realizing what I was saying. 'She's going to need all the love you can give her in the next few months.'

They just smiled at each other, so young and so very much in love, and Tony brushed her hair with his lips again. They didn't realize how seriously I meant it. But how could they? I didn't really know what I meant myself. All I knew was that every time I looked at Janet I wanted to go and put my arms round her and support her in some way. I was sure there was something wrong somewhere. Yet she looked the very picture of health and Ted said the doctors were very pleased with her.

Oh stop being fanciful, Stokes, I told myself sternly. You're imagining things. What you need is another cup of tea. And I went to fill the kettle, pushing that shadow firmly to the back of my mind.

Half an hour later as she left the theatre, Janet stumbled on an uneven paving stone and went straight over. Fortunately there was no harm done, but Ted and Tony, remembering my warning, made her take off her shoes then and there and walk the rest of the way to the car in her stockinged-feet. In a way I was relieved. Perhaps it was just the potential danger of her high heels that I'd picked up.

Weeks passed and at last came the news that the baby had been born. Janet had had a little girl and they were going to call her Hollie. Mother and baby were doing well we were told. It was good news, of course, but it didn't banish the feeling that there was something wrong somewhere. Every day, when I thought of the Roffeys and little Hollie that shadow seemed to grow stronger.

Well I'm not going to ring up and worry them, I told myself, you're just being over-imaginative because of John Michael. And it's true that after losing my own baby at 5 months, I've always mentally held my breath over other people's babies until they're a year old. It might seem illogical but I tend to feel that anything can happen in the first 12 months of life. Once a baby has reached a year I let out a sigh of relief and feel that he's safely on his way.

Then one day I opened the paper and there was a story about the baby who was to become the world's youngest heart transplant patient. It was a baby girl and her name was Hollie Roffey. The paper slipped from my fingers and with a cold sinking feeling, I realized that this was what I'd sensed from the start. Apparently at birth, Hollie had appeared quite normal and healthy but as the days went by her colour didn't look quite right and she was taken off for tests. The day Tony and Janet hoped to bring her home the results came through. They were told that the left side of Hollie's heart was missing. The defect was too drastic to attempt a repair. Hollie's only chance of survival was a heart transplant – if a suitable donor could be found.

Everybody worked very hard to save little Hollie. By the time I phoned Ted, a donor had been found and the family were at the hospital pacing the corridors and drinking strong coffee while the operation took place. Ted's son, Simon, answered the phone.

'Simon, I don't want to intrude,' I said, 'could you just tell your dad that I rang and that we're praying for Hollie.'

I don't know how the Roffeys got through the next few days. It was such a tense time. Little Hollie's plight touched the whole country. The newspapers, radio and television carried regular stories about her and her brave struggle for life melted the coldest hearts. Amazingly for such a fragile little thing she hung on for 17 days after the operation. She was a born fighter.

At one point she seemed to rally, she started to suck and all the signs were hopeful. The whole nation held its breath. The length and breadth of the country people were rooting for Hollie.

Tony and Janet had spent every day at the hospital but at last Hollie's condition was so encouraging they were persuaded to go home for a rest. Tragically, while they were away their baby took a turn for the worse and before they could get back to the hospital she was gone.

John and I were at the van when we heard the news. I wasn't surprised, yet at the same time it was a shock and I felt desperately sorry for poor Tony and Janet. I knew exactly how they must be feeling. It was the story of John Michael all over again.

I know some people back away from tragedy. They don't know what to say so they don't say anything at all and you even hear of people who will cross the road rather than face someone who's suffered a bereavement. Yet the strange thing is, if you do face it, the words come and it means so much to the bereaved to know that people care.

It didn't even occur to me not to get in touch. Sadly, I dialled Ted's number.

'Ted, I'm so very sorry,' I said when he answered.

At the sound of my voice he seemed relieved.

'Oh Doris. Tony and Janet are here with us now. Can we come? Can I fetch you?'

21

How could I refuse? Scarcely half an hour later Ted arrived and whisked us back to his home. I think he was very glad that John and I happened to be in Kent that day because he was finding it difficult to comfort Janet and Tony.

They were in a dreadful state as anyone would have been. I put my arms round them both, then I sat them down and tried to talk to them. I don't know how much of what I said actually got through but we talked for about 3 hours.

'Listen, darling, Hollie's not dead,' I said. 'And she's done more in her short life than all of us put together could do in ninety years. She's paved the way to show that these operations can be done on tiny babies. Thanks to her, who knows how many lives will be saved. Just be proud you were chosen to be her parents.'

It's odd how in times of tragedy people often focus on one tiny detail which seems to take on an importance out of all proportion to the greater horror of what has happened. With Tony it was his baby's hair. Distraught as he was he was particularly upset because they'd shaved Hollie's head.

'She was so beautiful, Doris,' he sobbed, 'but they shaved her head. Why did they have to cut off her hair?'

He didn't really want a medical answer, of course, though doubtless there was one.

'Look Tony it doesn't matter,' I said, 'she's beautiful again now. She's got all her hair again on the other side. That wasn't Hollie you saw when you went back to the hospital, just her old overcoat.'

I didn't even attempt to do a sitting for them. It was too soon. Grief is natural, it's part of the healing process and I think it's better to let it out and adjust a little to the loss before contacting a medium. In the Roffeys' case though the spirit world wanted to clear up that one small point.

Suddenly as I was speaking I felt a small jolt as

something was put on my lap. I looked down and there was Hollie. Now I love babies and they all look beautiful to me, but Hollie was one of the most beautiful children I've ever seen. She was gurgling happily to herself and her head was a mass of tiny red gold ringlets, glossy as a new conker.

'There, isn't she lovely?' said a woman's voice. 'Tell Tony he can take it from me that she's got all her hair back now and I'm looking after her.'

It was Tony's grandmother and I gladly passed the message on. Only one thing puzzled me. The red gold hair. Both Tony and Janet were dark and I'd have expected Hollie to be dark like them or else baby fair with the kind of hair that darkens as the child grows. Yet Hollie's hair was bold and distinctive and quite unlike her parents.

It was only a few days later when I met Tony's brother that I discovered the answer. As soon as I saw his deep copper head coming towards me I realized that the colour ran in the family, and for some reason had bypassed Tony.

But the Roffeys' ordeal was far from over. The baby's body was taken to the undertakers and Tony and Janet had arranged to see her there. They told me about this and they kept hovering round until at last I realized what they'd left unsaid.

'D'you want to ask me to go with you?'

They exchanged relieved glances. 'Would it be imposing too much to ask you?' said Tony.

'Not a bit, love. Come and pick us up when you're ready.'

Well, it was an experience I'll never forget. I couldn't believe it. We drew up outside a bike shop, and at the side was a window, bare but for a vase with a few dusty artificial flowers in it. In we went and a man emerged from the shadows at the back.

'We've come to look at our baby,' said Tony painfully while Janet clung to my hand.

'Oh yes,' said the man. 'Follow me.' And he led us

out through the back of the shop, across a yard filled with old bikes, to a desolate little room at the end.

'In there,' said the man standing back.

Tony and Janet, quite numb, didn't move. 'Would you go in first, Doris?' Janet whispered.

'Yes, all right love,' I said and I'm very glad I did. The first thing I saw as my eyes adjusted to the light was a tiny white box no bigger than a shoe box, and a dead carnation lying on the top. Fortunately before we left the van that morning I'd cut a white rosebud, just starting to open and, quick as a flash, I whipped off the carnation and laid the rosebud in its place. And then there were those two poor kids standing beside me, Tony repeating, 'It's not fair. It's just not fair,' over and over again while Janet sobbed her heart out.

There was nothing to be done, of course, there never is, and at last I kissed the poor cold, uncomprehending little face and touched Janet's arm.

'Come on, love,' I said gently. 'It's only her old overcoat. She's not there you know. She's safe and happy.'

And, finally, we persuaded them away from that dismal place and took them home.

There was still the funeral to be got through and I was dreading it. Tony and Janet wanted us to be there and we wouldn't let them down for the world, but the whole sad episode was bringing back such vivid memories of the loss of John Michael that I found it very painful. After all, one heartbreakingly small white box looks very like another and day and night I found myself reliving the worst moments of my life.

'Now look,' I told Tony and Janet just before the funeral. 'The worst part is when you see that little box disappear into the earth. Just keep telling yourselves that's not Hollie. Hollie's safe.'

But it was a heart-rending affair nevertheless. There was a terrible moment when two hefty men came into the chapel with this pathetic little white box carried on a canvas sling between them. There was something ludicrous about two such burly figures sharing such a tiny burden. Why couldn't one of them have simply carried the coffin in his arms I wondered? At John Michael's funeral we had a little fair, curly-haired boy carrying my baby's box in his arms. It was simple, touching and appropriate. You don't need pomp and ceremony for an innocent little baby.

Yet although it was sad, that funeral underlined what a special child Hollie was and how in just a few short days she'd won the affection of so many people. The church was packed and magnificent floral tributes poured in from all over the country. Hollie's grave looked as if it was set in a carpet of flowers and to that blazing sea of colour John and I added our own little contribution. We'd cut every bud from every white rose bush in our garden, wrapped them in a white doily and added a little card. 'To Hollie. You didn't know the world but the whole world knew you.'

Afterwards, back at Ted's home, Janet and I strolled in the garden as she tried to calm herself. It was a warm day and crowds of mourners drifted outside for some air. We walked slowly back and forth and suddenly through the chatter I distinctly heard:

'I don't care what you say. Hollie's not there. Read Doris Stokes' books. I'm telling you . . .'

I couldn't help smiling. How nice to know that my words hadn't fallen on deaf ears. I moved towards the speaker, a pleasant-faced, middle-aged man to thank him for his recommendation but just as I reached him he noticed me. His words died away, his jaw dropped and his skin went a little pale under his tan.

'B-b-b-but it's her. It's Doris Stokes. Where did you come from?' he stammered for all the world as if he thought I'd just materialized out of thin air.

'I came to the funeral,' I said, 'I'm a friend of the family.'

He looked relieved and his healthy colour returned.

'Well, Doris! how lovely to meet you. Come and talk to us.'

Janet and I joined the group and although I hadn't intended to work, the day had been too emotional already, I found that the man's wife had arrived unseen from the spirit world and wanted to send him her love.

'And give my love to our Mary,' she said, 'and as for him, tell him to talk to Mary. They haven't spoken for years.'

Apparently there had been some sort of family disagreement and the man had fallen out with his sister-in-law. As the years passed it became harder for either of them to break the ice and although they sometimes went to the same functions, they behaved as if they'd never met. It turned out that Mary was at the funeral too and the prompting from the other side was all they needed. Before the afternoon was over that man was crouched beside Mary's chair, sheepishly making up for years of silence.

Once people find out that I'm a medium they're usually full of questions and after a while one of the other men in the group, Micky Dallon who'd been listening quietly, finally plucked up the courage to raise a subject that must have been bothering him for some time.

'When my mother was dying I sat with her holding her hand,' he said, 'and at one point I wanted to jump up and shout for the doctor, but at the same time I didn't want to leave her. In the end I stayed with mum and she died. Ever since I've been wondering if I did the right thing. If I'd got the doctor then, perhaps we could have saved her.'

I shook my head vigorously.

'No, love. You were right to stay and comfort her. It wouldn't have made any difference who you called. If it was your mother's time to go over she had to go and no one could have prevented it.'

Micky seemed satisfied and the conversation moved

on but I couldn't concentrate on what they were saying. A woman had joined us and she was bending forward to whisper to me.

'Give my love to Micky,' she murmured.

'Who are you?' I asked.

'It's Lilian,' she said and she was gone.

'Sorry to interrupt,' I said quietly out loud, 'but I just got something for Micky. It's not much. Lilian sends her love, that's all.'

It was the tiniest of messages but the effect was amazing. The colour just drained from Micky Dallon's face and he went so white I thought he might faint.

'It's such an unusual name . . .' he blurted through pale lips, 'you could never have guessed my mother's name was Lilian . . .' and he blundered away to get a drink to steady his nerves.

There are two sequels to the story of Tony and Janet, one rather strange and inexplicable, the other perfectly explicable and down to earth but just as wonderful.

The first occurred during that same long hot summer. The Roffeys spent quite a lot of time with us in our mobile home and naturally the subject of Hollie came up frequently. Tony seemed to be particularly anguished. He couldn't come to terms with the tragedy at all.

'I believe you, Doris,' he said time and time again. 'I believe everything you say but if only they could give me a sign that my baby's all right, then I could rest.'

His words used to tear at me because I wanted to help but there was nothing I could do. I'm only human after all. I could pass on messages I heard, and tell him what I knew about life on the other side but as to signs that he could see for himself, well that was out of my hands entirely.

'Well, Tony, be patient,' was all I could advise. 'If they think you need a sign, perhaps they'll send you one. Who knows?'

A week or two later when my back was less painful I decided to get on with some housework around the van. I pulled out our nest of tables and was giving them a good polish when suddenly I dropped the duster in surprise. There on the table we used most, the pattern of the wood had re-arranged itself, that's the only way I can describe it – into the face of Jesus complete with beard and crown of thorns. The little picture was about four inches long and in the opposite direction to the grain and what's more it had certainly not been there before. I blinked, looked away, and looked back again but it was still there.

Quickly I went into the bedroom where John was hoovering and touched his arm. 'John switch it off and come and look at this and tell me what you see.'

Puzzled he followed me into the living-room. Without saying a word I pointed at the table. John looked, then frowned, looked away and looked back, just as I had done.

'It's the face of Jesus,' he said. 'That's what it looks like to me. But I've never noticed it before.'

It's very easy to let your imagination run away with you in cases like this and John and I are so closely attuned I couldn't be sure I wasn't influencing him, so we decided to call in other opinions.

'If anyone'll know what that table used to be like it's Phyllis and Doreen,' I said.

Phyllis and Doreen were two of our friends on the site who used to air the van and give it a quick going over before we arrived if we'd been away for some time. We invited them in and without mentioning what was going on we asked them to look at the table. Both spontaneously saw the picture of Jesus.

'Well I've polished these tables I don't know how many times,' said Phyllis, 'and I've never seen that before.'

Finally, when we'd heard enough exclamations of astonishment to know we weren't seeing things, we told the Roffeys. They came, looked, and Ted was so impressed he took the table away to be photographed.

'Well, Tony,' I said, 'I'm not saying it is – but you did ask for a sign . . .'

Several months passed before the second sequel. I was very busy with the arrangements for moving and with the tour and so quite a few weeks went by before I saw the Roffeys again. Then, just before Christmas I did a very exciting demonstration at the London Palladium (more of that later) and afterwards, to my delight, Tony and Janet walked into the dressing-room. They both looked well and much happier than the last time I'd seen them and I was instantly reminded of my parting words in the summer.

'Well this time next year I hope I'll be able to come and have a drink with you at your christening.'

Janet was still as slim and agile as ever and yet there was something about her . . .

'Yes the baby's on its way,' whispered a voice in my ear and I beamed at the kids.

'I'm still keeping the summer free for the christening,' I joked.

Tony laughed ruefully. 'No, Doris. I'm afraid you'll have to wait a bit longer. We've had no luck yet.'

I stared at him in surprise. 'But I'm sure they . . .' then I saw Janet frantically signalling behind his back and I stopped. 'Oh well never mind, love,' I finished lamely, 'it'll happen in good time.' And I left it at that. I didn't want to spoil Janet's surprise.

Sure enough, a few days later on Christmas morning, Tony came downstairs to find a plain white card amongst his brightly wrapped parcels.

'Dear Tony,' it said. 'Sorry you'll have to wait another 33 weeks for your present. Love Janet.'

Tony, who must have been celebrating rather freely the night before, didn't get it. 'Thirty-three weeks?' he said puzzled, 'why will I have to wait thirty-three weeks?'

'Because I'm pregnant you idiot!' cried Janet and the next second he was swinging her round, very gently, in delight. It was the best Christmas present they could have had.

Chapter Three

The garden of the mobile home was looking lovely as I showed Lady Michaela Denis Lyndsay round and all about us was the scent of roses. Roses are my favourite flower. We'd planted dozens of bushes when we bought the van and now they were all out and blooming like mad.

It was so beautiful that Michaela and I quite forgot the cameras whirring away in the background recording every move and we drifted towards the seat beside a glorious 'Blue Moon', chatting as if we were alone.

'Oh look!' I cried as we sat down. 'There's Minnie the mongoose!'

The late Minnie had been a very special pet of Michaela's and now I saw her as plain as I saw my roses, snuggled on the bench against Michaela's leg, a little ball of fur with a pointed face and bright eyes.

'Oh yes,' said Michaela in delight, 'I see her. She's often with me you know.' And she stroked Minnie's head fondly. I reached out to pat Minnie myself and as I did so I smiled up at the cameramen. This must make a lovely scene for them, I thought, what a bit of luck, and then I noticed that far from smiling back, they had turned distinctly white and nervous and were staring at the seat uneasily.

That was when it clicked. Of course, Minnie was invisible to them. They must have thought we'd gone stark raving mad, patting and talking to a patch of thin air!

I bet they won't forget that particular edition of *Forty Minutes* in a hurry! I was tremendously flattered when BBC2 rang to ask if they could make me the subject of the programme. As most people probably know the programme takes its name from the length of screen time allotted to it but it takes a great deal longer than forty minutes to make.

The documentary team seemed to follow me round for weeks filming everything, until in the end they became like members of the family and I hardly noticed the cameras at all. They filmed in our flat, in our mobile home, at public demonstrations and church services and even in Bert Weedon's garden. Bert Weedon of course is the guitarist who wrote and played the background music on my LP. They couldn't use half of what they'd filmed, of course, because they must have recorded hours and hours of material, but I was very impressed with the finished programme. They'd made an interesting, intelligible documentary out of a great hotch-potch of different topics.

They said they wanted to cover just about every aspect of my work and beliefs and they certainly did. To explain my spirit guide, Ramanov, they decided to focus on the name plate of the mobile home which we'd named in his honour and then show me explaining the origin of the name to Michaela.

I've known Michaela for years and since she happened to be in England at the time they thought it might be nice if she appeared. A lot of people remember the wonderful wild life programmes she used to make with her first husband Armand. When he passed over she married Sir William Lyndsay which is why she is now a titled lady. Sir William too is now on the other side and these days Michaela lives alone in Kenya surrounded by her beloved wild animals. What few people realize though, is that Michaela is also a medium and every year she comes to London to attend the SAGB dinner dance and visit her spiritualist friends.

Michaela and Minnie did eventually reach the screen but many other scenes did not. At one point the producer got quite excited about the news that I could do sittings over the telephone.

'D'you think you could do one for us this afternoon?'

he asked. 'If we pick a letter from your post bag could you phone them and do it straight away?'

'I can try,' I said.

So one of the team delved down my huge pile of letters and came up with a note which included a phone number. To make doubly sure that I knew nothing of the contents she even dialled the number herself and then passed me the receiver as the phone was answered.

'Hello,' I said to the woman at the other end. 'This is Doris Stokes. I believe you wrote to me asking for a sitting.'

'Oh yes,' she said.

'Well,' I explained, 'I can do one on the phone for you if you don't mind the BBC recording it. They're here now making a documentary.'

'Oh,' she said, 'what time?'

The producer signalled impressively.

'It's got to be half-past-one.'

'Oh dear,' said the woman, 'couldn't you make it four-thirty. I go to bingo at half-past-one.'

But the producer was adamant and the woman seemed reluctant to miss her bingo so another letter was drawn from the bag. This time I tuned in as they were dialling the number and instantly I heard the name Doug.

'Look I don't want to know what's in the letter,' I whispered, 'but just tell me, is the name Doug mentioned?'

They skimmed through it. 'Yes.'

Thank goodness for that. I'd contacted the right person and not someone connected with the TV crew. It's so easy to get crossed wires when there are a lot of people about, because their friends and relatives in spirit are often so close to them.

This time we were in luck. The woman on the line was only too delighted to help and 1.30 suited her perfectly. It turned out that Doug was her husband. He was only fifty-four and he'd died suddenly of a heart attack.

'Who's Jenny?' I asked.

'My daughter-in-law,' said the woman.

'Doug tells me that you were with Jenny when it happened.'

'Yes I was,' she agreed.

'They were out Christmas shopping,' said Doug. 'They were in Marks and Spencers' buying me a sweater when I passed. I tried to tell them not to bother because I wouldn't be needing it but I couldn't make them hear.'

The woman was dumbfounded when I told her what her husband had said.

'That's exactly what we were doing,' she gasped when she got over her astonishment. 'We were in Marks buying him a sweater! Oh I'm so glad he knew.'

Unfortunately Doug and his sweater never did reach the final programme, there simply wasn't time, but I'd like to let him know that he's not forgotten!

The demonstration I gave at Poplar fared better on the screen. I can't say that every message I gave was shown on the programme but a good proportion did make it. There was a lot of laughter that night and one message in particular tickled the audience. A pair of women were standing together at the microphone and one of their relatives – I think it was their father – was chatting away in my ear.

'And when they knocked the wall down it all went wrong,' he tutted.

'Are you doing some building work at home?' I asked them. 'He's saying something about a wall knocked down and everything went wrong.'

The women looked at each other and giggled.

'Yes!'

'What a mess,' the man went on. 'And when they got the tiles for the floor, there weren't enough!'

I passed this on and by now the women were practically in tears of laughter.

'Yes, but it wasn't the tiles, it was the glue we ran out of!' they corrected.

'Oh well, tiles, glue whatever, they ran out and had to rush off to the shop to get some more,' said the man. 'And at home they daren't move till the glue arrived. What a mess! I cleared off till it was all finished.'

There were the usual moments of confusion too, which I've learned I just have to put up with when I'm working with a big audience. I can normally tell who a message is intended for by the light I see shining close to them, but often there are so many spirit people eager to talk to their loved ones that the place is packed with lights. What's more the theatres are usually so crowded, with the seats packed so close, it's impossible to say exactly which person I'm looking for.

That night in Poplar, a woman called May told me she was looking for a young lady in a red dress. There was a light hovering near a woman in the front who seemed to fit the description.

'Yes that must be me!' she shouted eagerly hurrying forward.

But I wasn't certain. Something didn't seem quite right. In the background someone gave me the name Fred.

'D'you know someone called Fred, spirit side?' I asked.

She shook her head. She was the wrong contact. As soon as I mentioned the name Fred, Fred himself came in drowning May altogether.

'It's my daughter I want,' he said, 'and she's wearing red.'

Suddenly I was aware of a hand waving frantically near the back of the hall.

'I know a Fred,' she called.

'Are you wearing red, love?' I asked because, dazzled by the lights, I couldn't see the back.

'Yes I am,' she called and came running down to the microphone.

I wanted to make absolutely certain however that I'd

found the right person so I asked for further identification. 'Mention working for the Co-op,' he said.

'Who worked for the Co-op?' I asked.

'My father,' said the girl in wonder, 'he was a milk lorry driver.'

I breathed a sigh of relief. We'd found Fred's daughter.

'Tell her that Eva's here with me,' he said.

The girl gasped. 'That's my mother! They're together? Oh I'm so glad.'

'She's our baby,' said Fred and you could hear all the love and affection in his voice. They must have been very close. 'And she's wearing her mother's ring. She's got it on tonight.'

His daughter's smile was dazzling. 'Yes I have.'

All at once the crowded hall faded and before my eyes I saw a glorious lilac bush. Not the spindly, insignificant little tree that you see in so many gardens, but a really lush, magnificent shrub. Then the picture was gone. Now why had Fred shown me a lilac bush I wondered.

'You haven't got a lilac bush in your garden have you?' I asked the girl.

'Why yes. A really beautiful one.'

'That's it,' I said. 'They've just just shown me a beautiful lilac bush and they're saying when the lilacs are out in the spring cut a spray and say Mum and Dad's here.'

'Oh, thank you, I will,' she assured me her face lit with joy.

All evening the spirit people came flooding through. Some were marvellous communicators, others quite overcome by the excitement. One grandmother was so thrilled to be able to tell her daughter that she had seen the grandchildren she'd never lived to meet on earth that all she could do was babble their names over and over again. 'Rachel and Rebecca! Rachel and Rebecca!' she kept telling me in delight.

Another young lad who was killed in an accident

seemed to think that the name of his favourite pub was all the information necessary to convince his sister that he was really there.

'Just mention the Green Man,' he said confidently.

And some messages seemed puzzling to me but made perfect sense to the recipients. At one point I got the name Proctor and not one, but two ladies claimed it. It turned out they were the Proctor sisters, a bubbly duo full of fun.

'Well, this is very odd,' I told them, 'I've got a lady here, I'm sure it's a lady, but they're calling her Henry.'

The sisters collapsed into each other's arms all laughter and dimples. 'Yes that's right. It's Henrietta but Father always called her Henry.'

'And now I've got another lady but they're calling her George.'

The sisters could hardly speak for mirth. 'That's right,' they spluttered, 'Georgina!' and the whole theatre laughed with them.

The Proctor sisters were obviously enjoying themselves immensely. So much so that the next day when they were on a day trip to Clacton they decided to buy me a present. They'd read in my books that I'm specially fond of gold roses and passing a florist's they saw the very thing they were after. A pretty arrangement of roses in the very shade I'd described. The only snag was that the shop was shut but the Proctor sisters weren't going to be defeated by a tiny detail like that. They went all the way back to Clacton the next day and bought it.

Soon after the Poplar demonstration the Forty Minutes' team followed me to Deal where I was doing a church service. I try to attend a church as often as possible because I think it does me good. It reminds me what my work is all about. The big theatres and the assorted messages are only a small part of it. The rest is as much about living your life now, as life after death.

I must say our services are usually quite lively. We

have hymns and prayers, of course, like other churches but it's all very informal, not a bit holier than thou. Then when the religious part is over there's a short demonstration.

It was lovely to visit Deal. A pretty little town on the South coast with the salt tang in the air you always get by the sea and a fresh breeze blowing. The church was bright and welcoming and full of flowers and the congregation was squeezed in so tightly it's a wonder they had enough breath to sing!

After a relaxed service I did a demonstration. This was the time when I was suffering with my back and the actual details of the demonstration have faded, all I can recall is the dull ache that I hoped didn't show on my face. One thing does stand out though. A boy came through saying that he was connected with the navy and that he'd taken himself over. He was claimed immediately by a woman in the congregation but once again it seemed slightly off key. Many of the details didn't mean a thing to her and thought she was eager for the message to be hers I had an uneasy feeling I was talking to the wrong contact. But my back was aching, the heat was increasing and other spirit voices were jostling to be heard. So instead of working at it and trying to sort out the confusion as I normally do, I passed on to the next message. I might have known, however, that Ramanov wouldn't let me get away with such sloppiness.

After the service I noticed out of the corner of my eye a woman and young man approach the producer. They stood talking to him for some minutes and then he brought them over to me.

'They were so disappointed, Doris, not to get a message,' he said and the woman pressed a photograph into my hand.

'That's him, Doris,' she told me pleadingly.

She was a handsome blonde with clear, creamy skin but the expression in her blue eyes told me she'd lost a child. I looked at the picture. A smiling, suntanned

38

young man looked back at me and as I stared I realized
that he was with us.

'I'm here,' he said, 'I've been trying to get through.'

'What do I call you, son?' I asked silently.

'Stephen,' he said.

'I hear the name Stephen,' I told the couple and the
other boy clutched the woman's arm.

'That's him. That's my brother!' he said.

'He's wearing all my jewellery and stuff,' said Stephen, 'but I don't mind. It's no good to me now is it?'

'That's right I am,' cried the brother.

The woman's face lit up. 'He's been waiting for that
for a year,' she said. 'He used to be frightened of spirits
and things but he's read your books and he felt sure
you could help.'

The case was not a clear cut one though. Around
Stephen's passing I could sense a great deal of mystery
and confusion. It wasn't the sort of thing to be tackled
in five minutes before lunch I felt.

'Look,' I said impulsively. 'I think there's a lot to be
gone into here. I've got a day off tomorrow. Why don't
you come and see me at the van and we'll see what we
can do.'

They agreed eagerly and when we got started on the
sitting I was very glad I'd asked them to come back.

As soon as I tuned in, the feeling of confusion swept
over me more strongly than ever. This was no ordinary
accident victim or sufferer from an illness. This poor
mixed up boy had taken his own life.

I chose my words carefully in an attempt to spare
the mother's feelings.

'There's a great deal of mystery and confusion here,'
I said, 'Stephen wasn't killed, he was found.'

His mother bit her lip. 'Yes, I found him.'

I caught a fleeting glimpse of a teenage bedroom.

'You found him on his bed?'

She shook her head. 'No, on the floor in his bedroom.'

So that was why he'd shown me the room, but

Stephen wasn't quite ready yet to discuss the details. He was still ashamed to have caused his family so much pain and he kept shying away from the subject whenever I brought it up.

'Don't forget to remember me to Gary,' he said ignoring my question.

'Who's Gary?' I asked out loud.

'One of his best friends.'

I tackled Stephen again. 'Now look I know it's difficult love,' I told him silently, 'but I do need to know your last impressions. Can you just give me some idea what happened?'

All at once the confusion swamped me and there was an uncomfortable feeling in my head. My head hurt and my chest felt constricted.

'I feel as if I've got something over my head,' I said thinking aloud, 'and I can't breathe. Did he take an overdose or something?'

His mother shook her head. 'No he shot himself.'

I was surprised. The strange feeling in my head was a very strong impression. I don't deny that I sometimes make mistakes but when spirit people give me a clear impression it's never wrong. My interpretation of it may be way out but the impression itself is always correct.

'Well this feeling in my head seems very definite,' I insisted.

'It's funny you should say that Doris,' said Stephen's mother, 'because for a couple of weeks before he died he'd been complaining about his head.'

'I'd got it into my head there was something wrong,' said Stephen, 'I must have been mad. What a stupid thing to do. But it felt as if the top of my head was coming off. I thought I was ill.'

Then he gave me the name Joan.

'Who's Joan?' I asked.

'I am,' said his mother beaming.

Stephen went on to tell them that he played the

40

guitar on the other side, which pleased them very much.

'He always wanted to play the guitar,' said his brother, 'he used to stand in front of the mirror and pretend.'

Stephen also started talking about a dinner service which puzzled me rather because young men aren't usually bothered about things like that. It wasn't at all clear though and I wasn't sure what he meant.

'Why's he talking about a dinner service?' I asked.

'He's saying it's connected with work. You know plates and things, he's saying.'

His brother was thrilled. 'I think he means me. I've just started work as a steward. I work with plates and things.'

Finally, right at the end of the sitting I realized it had been Stephen trying to get through during the service in Deal with the message about the navy. He was talking about his funeral and he wanted to thank his family for the anchor of flowers they'd given him. It turned out that his father was in the navy. I'd found the right contact at last!

Not long after the *Forty Minutes* documentary, I had another phone call from the BBC, but this time it was from BBC Radio 2. Would I like to do *Desert Island Discs*? they asked.

For a minute I thought there must be some mistake, because surely they only have highbrow people on *Desert Island Discs*? But no, they said, they were quite certain they wanted Doris Stokes the medium. All I had to do, they explained, was pick out eight of my favourite records, records which meant something special to me, and talk about them.

Well it seemed easy enough and I love music. But when it actually came to narrowing down my favourites to just eight tunes it turned out to be more difficult than I'd imagined. Just when I thought I'd been really ruthless and pruned down my list as far as I could go,

I'd suddenly think of a really lovely piece I'd forgotten that I couldn't manage without.

It took me days. I got through pages of my writing pad with lists, revised lists and endless crossings out. But at last I settled on eight lovely tracks.

Presenter Roy Plomley, and producer, Derek Drescher, were lovely men. They invited John and I out to lunch to plan the programme but I explained that we don't really feel comfortable in posh restaurants.

'We just can't manage a big meal in the middle of the day,' I told Roy. 'We'd really much prefer tea and sandwiches in the office if it's all the same to you.'

So tea and sandwiches it was and we spent a lovely hour listening to all my discs and picking out the bits they were going to play because, of course, they can't play the records right the way through. Then it was time to record the programme with me talking to Roy between the music.

'I warn you I can woffle,' I told them but they thought I was joking.

'I'd sooner have a woffler than someone who doesn't say a word,' said Roy and away we went.

We started on a light note. Roy asked if I played a musical instrument and I explained that I didn't, though I'd always wanted to and I was hoping to learn in the spirit world.

'What will you play?' asked Roy. 'A harp?'

My first record was *One Day At A Time Sweet Jesus*. I go for the words every time and this song sums up how I've learned to live my life since I had cancer. Next was *I Love You Just Because* for John, because he's always there and when I'm tired or ill I don't always remember to let him know how much I appreciate it. *Morning Has Broken*, because it's such a beautiful song and it captures the pleasure I feel to see each new morning. Then there was *Mother Kelly's Doorstep* which always makes me smile because whenever I hear it, it reminds me of the time Danny La Rue came on stage at Birmingham Odeon to help me hand out flowers

42

and got me singing a duet with him of *Mother Kelly's Doorstep*. Now I can't sing a note, there's no two ways about it but the audience loved it. I think they treated it as a comedy routine!

After that there was Freddie Starr singing *Have I Told You Lately That I Love You* because whenever he phones, he serenades me with this song. Then I changed the mood completely and played *May The Good Lord Bless and Keep You*. Some people might think my reasons for choosing this rather sad but I don't. When I pass over I'm going to be cremated and I'd like this song played for my family because I'll be all right. I'll be away and happy with my loved ones on the other side. It's the ones who're left behind who will need help and comfort.

Finally I ended with *My Way* followed by my own reading of the poem that was given to me when I was mourning the death of my baby John Michael: *In a Baby Castle*. The words brought me such comfort at the time that I like to pass them on to every mother grieving for a lost child, in the hope they'll do the same for her as they did for me.

And then suddenly it was all over. The programme was recorded and I realized I'd been enjoying myself immensely.

Derek Drescher's head appeared round the door. 'That went on a bit too long, Roy,' he said.

I laughed. 'Well I did warn you I can waffle.'

And Roy, bless him, just grinned and leaned across the desk. 'Ah, but such magical waffle,' he said.

I seem to have been involved in a lot of programmes lately but with one of the most recent, *Glass Box*, which is only shown in the Granada TV area, I wasn't sure if I'd make it on to the screen at all.

Glass Box is recorded at the TV studios in Liverpool and it's a sort of visual *Desert Island Discs*. The idea is that you select a number of film clips that you particularly enjoy or that remind you of some special moment in your life and instead of taking them to an imaginary desert island, you seal them into a glass box to preserve them for ever.

I'd met the presenter, Shelley Rohde, before and we got on well and after enjoying *Desert Island Discs* so much I knew I'd enjoy *Glass Box*. I was looking forward to it. The choosing of the film clips had not been so difficult for me because films somehow don't seem to have such sentimental associations. There were some clips from the *Dambusters* to remind me of my airforce days, a piece from *Yield to the Night* with Diana Dors to remind me of our friendship and everyone else what a wonderful actress she was, some beautiful ballet because I've only recently learned to appreciate it and finally a scene from a horror movie because horror movies make me laugh so much. The whole thing would be great fun, I was sure.

Unfortunately, though, Liverpool went wrong from the evening we arrived. Some time before, a little girl of ten had written me a touching letter. She'd lost her Daddy she told me and she knew I could speak to him because she'd read my books. Could her Mummy bring her to see me because she wanted to tell her Daddy she loved him? I saw from the address that she didn't live too far from Liverpool and I realized that we might be able to combine a meeting with the *Glass Box* trip, so I asked Laurie to see if he could arrange for her to come and see me at the hotel.

This he did. 'But do remember to be there by six o'clock,' he said, 'because Doris has to go out at half-past-seven.'

We were meeting the producer of *Glass Box* to plan the next day's show and it was something that couldn't be put off.

Well we waited and waited. Six o'clock came and went and there was no sign of the little girl and her mother. At six-thirty I was convinced.

'They're not coming, Laurie, I'm certain of it,' I said.

'But they must be, they were so keen,' he insisted. 'Perhaps they're stuck in traffic somewhere.'

We waited until seven o'clock and then I had to get changed.

'Give me a shout if they arrive and I'll see if I can do something quick,' I said, 'but I've got a feeling Laurie. They're not coming.'

By half-past-seven even Laurie was forced to admit I was right. And it wasn't until the next night that we discovered what went wrong. They'd got the dates mixed up and come a day late. By the time they arrived in Liverpool I was almost home. I felt so sorry for that poor little girl. She'd been looking forward to talking to her Daddy and it had ended in disappointment. I'm still hoping we can meet one day.

The mishaps continued. That evening, no sooner had the meeting ended than Laurie hurried away to bed. It's most unusual for Laurie because normally he's a night owl, but his face was pale and drawn, despite the fact that he was complaining of the heat.

'Aren't you feeling too good, Laurie?' I asked, 'you don't look well.'

'Oh I'm fine, fine,' he insisted because he hates to admit to being ill. 'I only need a good night's sleep.'

'Looks like the 'flu to me,' said John when he'd gone.

'But it came on so suddenly,' I pointed out. 'He was all right at the meeting.'

We fully expected to find no sign of Laurie at breakfast the next morning but there he was, as bright and cheerful as if nothing had happened.

'Yes I'm fine now,' he said. 'But oh did I feel rough last night. At one point my legs just went to jelly. I could hardly stand up.'

Well, apart from shaking our heads over the peculiar bugs that go around these days we thought no more about it. Liverpool was like the North Pole that day with a wind that must surely have been blowing from a glacier and the weather was the main topic of conversation.

Earlier Laurie had taken a short stroll to the studio to check one or two points. It was only up the road from our hotel but the cold was so intense he couldn't face the walk back and had to take a taxi instead!

'Well if it's as bad as that I'm certainly not walking.' I said, 'I'll be blue by the time I get there!'

So at mid-day we climbed into our immaculate limousine for the two minute journey. They were very kind at the studio and had laid on a beautiful lunch in the directors' dining-room. Everyone tucked in hungrily except Shelley Rohde and I. Neither of us could eat a thing before working so we just pushed our food around on our plates and watched the others.

Then at last the meal was over and I was taken away to be made up. But half way down the stairs I went all dizzy and I swayed towards the make-up girl who was leading the way.

'I'll have to hold on to your shoulder, love,' I explained. 'I've come over a bit dizzy. I expect it's the heat.'

For it was very warm in the studio after the icy weather outside.

And settled in the comfortable chair in front of the big make-up mirror I felt fine. The girl soothingly combed my hair and put in heated rollers and then she put my face on. I did look a bit pale I thought but the foundation cream soon cured that.

At last, five minutes before I was due on the studio floor, I popped into the ladies. I was all ready. I've only got to slip into my dress and I can go on I was thinking, when suddenly without warning my legs went to jelly and my head spun. Anxiously I grabbed at the wall to steady myself. I was so dizzy I didn't think I could stand upright let alone walk coolly into a TV studio and talk intelligibly for half an hour.

Panic rising I waited for the attack to pass, but it didn't. My God, I thought, here I am with my make-up on and everything and I'm not going to be able to do it. They'll be calling me any minute and I don't think I can even get out of the loo.

In desperation I sent out a prayer to the spirit world.

46

'Please spirit friends just see me through this bit. Just see me through this hour. I don't mind what happens afterwards if I can just get this show done.'

And as always they turned up trumps. Even before I'd finished the prayer my head started to clear and my legs felt a little stronger.

By the time they called me to the studio I was wobbly and going hot and cold, but I was upright and walking and I got through that show as if there was nothing wrong with me.

The only one who had any idea was Shelley Rohde.

'You're not feeling very good are you, Doris?' she said afterwards.

'Oh dear, was I dreadful?' I asked.

'Not at all, it went marvellously,' she said. 'No one else noticed a thing. It's just that we're old friends and I could tell.'

And in fact when I saw a tape of the show afterwards I was relieved to see she was right. I don't look my best I'll admit. I look rather tired and drawn about the eyes and despite the make-up my colour's not good. But I don't think anyone would know that only five minutes before the cameras started rolling I could hardly stand up, let alone make light-hearted conversation.

The mystery bug hadn't finished with me of course and the journey back to London was pretty miserable but I couldn't complain. I'd asked the spirit world for the strength to see me through the show and they'd given me exactly what I'd asked.

People often comment about how frequently I seem to fall ill. Well all I can say is I'm as fed up about it as anyone I can tell you! I can't understand why I seem to be so unlucky in that respect. I can only think it's the spirit world's way of forcing me to slow down when I'm doing too much.

Yet ironically when I appeared on the Wogan show it wasn't me who was ill – it was Terry Wogan!

I was filled with trepidation when I first received the invitation to appear on the show. After all Terry can be a bit, well not sarcastic exactly, but cheeky with his guests and I thought I might be an ideal target. Nevertheless I've always had a soft spot for Terry Wogan. I think he's a gorgeous man and so I couldn't help but agree to go on his show just to get the chance to meet him!

I'd been keeping my fingers and toes crossed that I wouldn't get a cold or anything before the show and I was in luck. But when I arrived at the studio poor old Terry was all flushed and snuffling and struggling to get through the show despite a nasty bout of 'flu.

He gave me a terrific build up – psychic superstar and goodness knows what else – and then when I walked on he took both my hands in his and kissed my cheek. Well, even at my age it sent shivers up my spine!

'Terry,' I said when we sat down, 'before you start I must say that I think you're gorgeous – and I'm old enough to be able to say it!'

He looked at me with that wicked twinkle in his eye but he was very good. He asked me sensible questions and let me answer them. He was tickled to death when I told him about the Sod It Club – the club I'd formed with fellow cancer sufferers with one aim in mind – to say sod it, I'm not going to have it, to the dreaded 'C'.

Terry rocked back in his chair when I explained that Sod It didn't stand for anything, it simply meant sod it.

'I thought it was to do with psychic things!' laughed Terry.

Our interview lasted fourteen minutes I'm told and I enjoyed every second of it. Afterwards we met Terry again in the hospitality suite and I realized that he wasn't at all well.

'Why don't you spend the weekend in bed love?' I asked.

'I wish I could, Doris,' said Terry, 'but I've got to work.'

It was a very happy evening. What I particularly

liked about the programme was that every guest had a person to look after them throughout. They met you at the door, took you to your dressing-room, then on to make-up. They took you to the set, waited for you to come off and then took you back to the hospitality suite. It really made you feel they were pleased to have you on the programme.

All that and Terry Wogan too!

Chapter Four

The demonstration was going well. I was standing on the stage at Birmingham Odeon, the audience seemed to be enjoying themselves and the voices were coming through thick and fast. Once again, though I'd been tired earlier in the evening, energy seemed to flow from nowhere and I was skimming along on a wave of psychic power getting through more work than I'd have thought possible a few years ago.

'I'd like to ask a question,' said a neat little lady at the microphone on the floor below me.

'Go ahead, love,' I told her.

'I'm a widow and I'd like to know if my husband knows I go to the graveyard every week and that every time I go there's this little robin. If he's not there when I arrive, he comes soon afterwards and I take him something to eat.'

I was just about to tell her that I was sure her husband knew, because our loved ones stay close to us and continue to take an interest in all our activities, when a scornful Brummie voice interrupted my thoughts:

'Does she think I've come back as a bloody *bird*?' he asked.

Well I burst out laughing and when I explained why, the audience roared. The woman giggled too.

'Yes but I'll tell you something strange,' she said as the laughter subsided. 'Before he went over we used to discuss things and I used to say when I go over I'm going to come back as a bird so I can poop on all the people who pooped on me in my life!' (Sorry about that but that's exactly what she said.)

Anyway the audience fell about and the atmosphere which was already happy became almost euphoric.

Well I like to share everything that happens with the audience and I thought this story was fun, so the following night when I was appearing at the Odeon again, I told them about the robin, only I thought I'd better clean up the punch line a bit.

'. . . and she said, "I'd like to come back as a bird so that I can **** on all the people who **** on me in my life," ' I quoted.

As I expected, the audience roared, but as the commotion died away I saw a neat figure waving wildly from the front row. It was the little widow.

'I'm here, Doris! I've come again!' she shouted. Then she turned round to the rest of the audience: 'It's quite true. Every word – only I didn't say ****. I said "so that I can poop on all the people who *pooped* on me!" '

And of course the theatre practically exploded.

Yes we have a lot of fun one way and another. I think people who come along to demonstrations for the first time are quite surprised. They expect gloom and doom and instead they get jokes and laughter. There are tears as well, of course, but they are tears of joy and emotional release, not sorrow.

Sometimes it's the spirit people who say funny things. During one demonstration I'd been talking to a man on the other side for some time when suddenly he said rather mischievously, 'Mention the mountain goat.'

I thought my powers were going peculiar.

'Mountain goat?' I queried silently. 'Did you say mountain goat?'

The man assured me that he did.

It was one of the unlikeliest messages I've ever been asked to pass on but he was insistent, so feeling a bit of a fool I took a deep breath.

'Well I don't know if this means anything to you, dear,' I said, 'because it sounds strange to me, but he's saying something about a mountain goat.'

To my surprise the girl just fell apart. 'You couldn't

have given me better proof,' she said. 'That's what we used to call my father-in-law – the mountain goat!'

Sometimes the messages leave me tongue-tied because they're so forthright. I stand there dithering and stalling while I try to translate them into a tactful phrase. After all I don't want to embarrass anybody.

'Will you tell my daughter to make up her mind,' said one irate mother. 'She's living with two men. One's on nights and one's on days.'

Well how could I say that out loud in front of hundreds of people?

Just as often though, it's the people who're still with us on this side who provide the fun. Not long ago we did a book signing session in a big Midlands store. Afterwards we ran through the rain to the car and as I got in I noticed a very pretty blonde lady beckoning to John.

He went over to see what she wanted and she took his arm and walked him up the car park. The next thing we saw, she had her raincoat open and John had his head inside.

Laurie and I exchanged glances. 'What on *earth* is my husband doing!' I exclaimed.

A few minutes later John came trotting innocently back. 'She's got a cut-out under there!' he said climbing into the car and grinning from ear to ear.

'You dirty old man!' said Laurie.

John looked puzzled. 'Why? What have I done now?'

'We saw you with your head in her coat,' teased Laurie, 'and now you tell us she had a cut out dress.'

'Cut out dress?' said John in surprise. 'She didn't have a cut out dress. She had a cut-out of Doris.'

And he looked so wounded we couldn't help laughing. Back at the bookstall we'd noticed a few large cardboard cut out photographs of me on a stand and this lady had obviously whipped one and smuggled it out of the shop under her coat.

We were still laughing as we swung out of the car

park. We rounded a bend and there on a traffic island in the middle of the road was the blonde and a few of her friends, waving this cut-out over their heads and chanting, 'Doris Stokes! Doris Stokes!' just like a football crowd. They waved merrily as we went by and we all waved back.

What they made of our car I don't know. Since Laurie has been looking after us we've taken to travelling long distances in grand style. We often have to travel hundreds of miles to an appointment and in the past when we had to go by train and taxi I've arrived so exhausted by the journey I've not been sure whether I'd have enough energy left to work. Laurie changed all that.

'You can't do your job if you're worn out by travelling,' he said, 'you need to travel in as much comfort as you can.'

And he promptly hired us a grand midnight blue Daimler, complete with TV, telephone and cocktail cabinet for our next long journey. We've used it on our tours ever since. It's the most beautiful car you've ever seen and I feel like the Queen rolling up at theatres in it. I suppose we must look very impressive as we bowl along the motorways, but what other motorists don't see is that we're sitting there with our shoes off and our feet up, eating tuna fish sandwiches, drinking tea out of paper cups and singing our heads off. It's the only way to cover the miles. If we didn't have a laugh and a sing-song we'd go mad.

'You don't drink *tea* out of paper *cups*!' said one horrified friend. 'You should have champagne in a car like that.'

But we'd sooner have tea than champagne any day and we're not interested in the car as a status symbol. It's simply the next most comfortable thing to my armchair at home. Mind you, although I'm not out to impress anyone, I had to laugh at the reaction of an old cousin of mine recently.

We happened to be in my home town of Grantham,

and this cousin I hadn't seen for years, came up. We chatted for a while catching up on old times and when it was time to go he walked out to the car with us.

The sight of the limousine nearly took his breath away.

'Ee, is this what you came in, Dol?' he asked.

I assured him it was.

He walked round it a couple of times, ran a reverent hand over the gleaming bodywork and peered through the window for a look at the palatial interior.

'I say, Dol, is that a TV you've got in there?'

I nodded.

'And is that a telephone?'

I had to agree that it was.

The information took a second or two to sink in and even then he clearly found it difficult to believe.

'Ee,' he said at last, shaking his head, 'bloody 'ell you could live in there!'

Yes the last few years have brought a great deal of fun but it wouldn't be true to say the growing fuss hasn't brought problems as well. I find the letters very worrying. Every week I get literally hundreds of letters. Soon after we moved to our new house I breathed a sigh of relief because there had been no mail that morning. But I spoke too soon. Minutes later there was a knock at the door. It was the post girl.

'Could I possibly have a drink of water,' she said, 'I've almost finished then I'm going home for the pram.'

The pram? I thought. Surely she wasn't going to bring a baby out in this weather. It was bitterly cold and there was a freezing wind.

'Oh no,' she said, 'it's for your post. There's so much I can't carry it all so I'm going to put it in the pram and wheel it round.'

You can see the problem. I get pram loads of mail every day. If I spent each day doing nothing but answering letters I still wouldn't finish them and the next morning there would be another batch. It's impossible to deal with. What's more, the letters themselves are heartrending. Each has a tragic story. Every correspondent starts by saying they know I'm very busy and that I can't see everyone and then goes on to explain why they should be a special case. The trouble is, I know everyone's a special case but I can't see everyone.

Sometimes it makes me despair. There's so much sadness out there and I want to help but I feel as if I'm trying to empty the ocean with a tea cup.

Even more of a worry are the people who get fed up with waiting for a reply and come calling instead. A couple of weeks ago I had my first day off in two months. It was a wonderful luxury. Our glamorous hire car might seem like the height of good living to some people, but for me there is no greater luxury than sitting at home with absolutely nothing to do.

Right, I thought, that morning. I'm not going to do a thing. I'm not going to talk to anyone, tune in to anyone, I'm not even going to open a letter. I'll just sit in my chair and watch a bit of television. But I must have been more exhausted than I knew, because no sooner had the programme started than I fell asleep. John woke me up with a sandwich at lunch time but afterwards I drifted off again.

All around me I was vaguely aware of the sounds of the house, but they could have been a thousand miles away. Then at some point in the afternoon I heard a bell ringing.

'Oh it's the phone,' I thought sleepily. 'John'll get it.'

But it wasn't the phone, it was the front door and I was abruptly woken by John leading a complete stranger into the room.

'I thought you'd better see her, love,' he said. 'She's come a long way.'

Apparently this lady had set out from Hertford early

that morning determined to find me despite the fact she didn't have my address. She'd read in the books that I lived in some disabled ex-servicemen's flats and she was under the impression they were in the Kensington area, so she went to Kensington and walked the streets looking for the flats and asking if anyone knew of them.

At last a newsagent told her he thought the place she was looking for might be in Fulham and he told her which bus to get because Fulham is quite a distance from Kensington. But the lady was too impatient to wait for a bus. She ended up walking all the way to Fulham and after more tramping about she found the flats. Now there are a great many flats in the complex where we used to live. There are several long blocks, each block four storeys high, but undaunted, she started knocking on doors until she stumbled across one of the three people who knew my new address and persuaded them to give it to her. Then she caught two trains and walked another fair step, until she reached my door.

What could I do? I was not at all pleased, but after such a long journey I felt I had to give the poor woman a cup of tea. The one thing I wouldn't do though was give her a sitting. There was a time when under similar circumstances I'd have relented but not any more. Now I realize that it wouldn't be fair to all those people patiently and politely waiting, some of them for two years, on the waiting list. So I chatted to this lady, gave her tea and let her phone her family because they'd had no idea what she was up to and she'd be very late home and then I gently explained that we were about to start our supper and she would have to go.

I felt a bit guilty about it afterwards but also annoyed. Why should someone make me feel guilty about having a day off? It wasn't fair. Even vicars are allowed time off. I'm sixty-five years old now and surely I'm entitled to a rest now and then.

The great ocean of grief all around is just too much for me to handle so I've had to be sensible. Now I concentrate on mass demonstrations because I can give a lot of people a little comfort in the time it used to take me to comfort one. As for private sittings, I still do a few, but I let the spirit world guide me. They let me know which people are most in need of help which people I must see. Sometimes I'm going through a sack of mail and one letter will literally leap into my hand. Occasionally the feeling of urgency is so strong that I immediately drop what I'm doing and phone the sender right away, although it's not always clear to me why speed is so important. Sometimes the sender will be a distraught mother almost out of her mind with grief over a lost child, but other cases are less straightforward.

One morning I was sifting through the mail as usual when a small envelope addressed in a round childish hand almost flew into my lap. It was from a sixteen-year-old girl in Scotland who'd recently lost her much loved Nanna. A sad but not unusual story you might think but there was more to it than that. From the other side there was a great rush of urgency and I got the impression of a woman trying to push me to the phone.

I looked at the signature on the letter. The girl's name was Cheryl and she obviously needed help. I put down the rest of my postbag and dialled the number she'd printed beneath her address.

Cheryl herself answered the phone and once she'd got over the surprise, the sad story came pouring out. Brought up chiefly by her grandmother she'd been devastated when the old lady died. Now she was unhappy at home. She didn't get on with her step-father and to comfort herself she'd started eating vast amounts of food.

'She always was a big girl,' said a strong Scots voice in my other ear, 'but now she's gone up to nineteen stone and she won't go to school. She won't leave the house. It's such a waste.'

Cheryl admitted it was true. 'I can't go to school. The other kids laugh at me because I'm so fat,' and she started to cry.

I realized that if something wasn't done quickly there could be another tragedy.

'Now, Cheryl, listen to me,' I said, 'you're making your Nan very unhappy. She's here now and she's telling me you're such a beautiful child she can't bear to see you letting yourself go. If only you'd lose some weight and make yourself smart, everyone would want to know you and you wouldn't want to hide away at home.'

'If you'd just stop buying sweets and biscuits and nibbled at an apple or a carrot when you were hungry you'd soon lose weight. If you do that, I promise you that before the year's over you'll be having a wonderful time. You're only sixteen for goodness sake. Your Nanna wants to be a great-grandmother and she's not going to do that if you're shut up in the house . . .'

Cheryl sniffed and sobbed but eventually she agreed to try a diet.

'It's not easy, Cheryl,' I said, 'I've got thyroid trouble and I'm sixty-five and I have to be really strong with myself or I'd be twenty-one stone. But your Nanna says there's nothing physically wrong with you – it's just insecurity. So if you could just stick to a diet for a few months you'd see the weight roll off.'

Cheryl promised to do her best and I gave her my phone number so that she could ring me with progress reports or just for a chat if she felt desperate.

'And remember, Cheryl,' I added at the end of the conversation, 'when things get difficult just put out your hand and your Nanna will be there to help you. She's not far away and she's watching over you.'

Afterwards I could only pray that I'd got through to that poor child and helped her back on the path to a normal life. The spirit world had done their bit, I'd done mine, and now it was up to Cheryl to find the strength to pick up the pieces.

Occasionally, however, my post bag brings me news of even more disturbing matters. Another of the letters that forced itself to my attention contained a very alarming story. It was from a woman whose hotel business was almost ruined despite the 'advice' I'd been giving her for so long through a 'mutual friend'. She wanted to thank me for the work I'd done on her behalf, but she'd now sadly come to the conclusion that the business was beyond redemption.

Horrified, I skimmed through the letter again. I had never heard of this lady or her hotel and the name of our 'mutual friend' meant absolutely nothing to me. What on earth was going on? This time I didn't need the spirit world to prompt me. I was instantly on the phone.

'Oh thank goodness you phoned,' said this poor woman when I explained who I was and that I was quite mystified by the whole thing. 'It was my daughter who suspected there was something wrong. She read your books and then she read your predictions and she said you know Mum these sound as if they were written by two different people. There's just no comparison.'

'Predictions?' I asked more alarmed than ever. 'What predictions? I don't make predictions I'm not a fortune teller.'

'Oh yes this friend says she knows you and that she regularly visits you to discuss people's problems and that you make predictions about what they have to do. Just a minute, I'll read you some.'

She went away and came back with a piece of paper.

'It says here, "I, Doris Stokes, do hereby declare . . ." ' and she went on to read out the worst load of rubbish I've ever heard. It included instructions to sweep up the leaves from the hotel yard, put them in a jar and keep them in the bathroom. This utter nonsense was apparently signed with my name and these so called messages from me had been arriving almost every month for some time.

'I feel such a fool now,' said the poor woman, 'but she was so plausible. She described you and your home. She even said things like, "d'you like my dress? Doris Stokes gave me this." We followed all her instructions thinking they came from you and now we're just about ruined.'

I was appalled. 'But I've never met this woman in my life,' I said. 'She's probably seen me and my flat on television or in pictures.'

There was little I could do to help save their business. I could only sympathize and suggest they throw away the dead leaves in the bathroom and anything else I was supposed to have instructed them to collect. Finally I asked for the address and telephone number of our 'mutual friend'. She must be stopped. How could people be so wicked? And how many other people was she ruining in my name?

Furiously I dialled the number and got through right away. My 'old friend' sounded quite taken aback to hear from me.

'Now look,' I said, 'I've never met you, I've never spoken to you and you've never been to my home.'

'Eh. Well. No. But we have met,' said the woman faintly.

'Where?' I demanded, 'I don't recall ever meeting you.'

'We met in a previous life,' she insisted, but I think it sounded ridiculous even to her.

Well I'm afraid I told her what I thought of her. I told her that her friend would probably lose the hotel and that what she'd done was quite wicked.

'And how many other people have you been sending predictions to?'

She hesitated. 'Eh well, not many. I only do it to comfort them you know. I didn't mean any harm.'

I was too angry to think straight at that, so I brought

the conversation to an end intending to ring back when I'd cooled down. From then on, however, the phone was permanently engaged. In the end I had to be content with sending a strongly worded solicitor's letter forbidding her to pass on any more messages in my name.

The lengths people will go to and the nonsense they are prepared to come out with constantly amazes me. Why they do it I can't imagine. Perhaps they're trying to get attention, perhaps they've got problems, but whatever the reason they've got no right to take advantage of gullible people looking for help.

A newspaper rang me recently to ask if I could help with a reader's query. This woman had written in to say that her husband had gone missing and she'd consulted a medium to find out if he was dead or alive. The medium had taken her money and told her that the husband was definitely on the other side but that he couldn't talk to her because he'd been killed by a blow to the head and he was delirious. The newspaper wanted to know if this was possible! Now I ask you? It would be funny if it wasn't so serious.

Another woman sent me a tape recording of a sitting she'd had with a so called medium who had spent most of the time singing hymns.

'I was so upset and felt so dreadful after that sitting,' she wrote, 'that I felt like coming out and throwing myself under a bus.'

As I read the letter I heard the name Mark, very clearly, so I phoned her straight away.

'I'm so sorry you had such a bad experience,' I said, 'but as I was reading your letter I heard the name Mark and I knew it was important.'

'Yes that's right. That's what I was waiting for. Mark's my son.'

'Well, love, he took himself over didn't he,' I said because Mark had just told me he was very ashamed of what he'd done.

'Yes he did,' she admitted in astonishment.

'And he tells me he did it away from this country.'

'Yes.'

'Tell them I'm sorry,' Mark begged me, 'I hadn't been married very long.'

'Only four months,' sobbed his mother, but despite the overwhelming emotion she was pleased. 'That's all I wanted,' she said. 'That's why I went to a medium in the first place. I didn't want to bother you because I know you're busy, but I felt so dreadful after this other sitting. It was awful. All I wanted to do was get out. I felt sick.'

She was quite content with the few scraps I was able to give her but I felt very sad that she'd been treated so badly, especially by a person who called herself a medium.

Sometimes I just don't understand people at all.

I suppose the most depressing reading of all though, comes through the letter box every morning in the shape of the newspaper. Is it just my imagination or is the news getting worse? Every day people seem to think of new and more horrible ways of being nasty to each other. But at least now I have a little money behind me I sometimes get the chance to put right, in a very small way, a few wrongs.

Some months ago I was upset to read about a poor little boy who was set upon by louts who smashed his expensive hearing aid. How they could be so cruel to a child who has enough problems to contend with anyway, I don't know, and my heart went out to the little boy. He must be so confused and disillusioned with life.

Impulsively I sat down and wrote him a note. I promised to buy him a new hearing aid and added; 'Just to tell you there aren't all nasty people in the world – there are some nice people too, people who love you and want you to be happy.'

I couldn't undo the pain and misery he'd gone through but perhaps I could cheer him up a little, and help restore his faith in human nature.

It's worth all the hard work and tiring journeys to be able to make little gestures like these and I know my dad would be pleased. As he used to say to me when I was a girl: 'If you want to keep love, Dol, you have to give it away.'

Chapter Five

Diana Dors was unmissable. There she was, large but glamorous in a sleeveless black dress, her blonde hair falling round her shoulders, her long, long, eyelashes almost brushing the glass in her hand and her infectious laugh brightening everybody in the room. The place was packed and all the guests had dressed up, yet it was Diana you noticed. The slender figure of the fifties sex symbol might have disappeared for ever but Diana was still every inch a star.

John and I were a bit over-awed to tell the truth, so we just said a polite hello as we passed and moved on to mingle with the other guests. It was certainly a splendid do. Robert Maxwell who owns the company which publishes my books had invited all his authors to a reception at his beautiful old home, Headington Hill Hall near Oxford. It was a magnificent house, built like a castle with a massive staircase and a minstrel gallery, and the Maxwells had gone to endless trouble over the arrangements. A toastmaster announced the guests as they entered the solid oak door; there were waiters circulating with trays of champagne and wine and there was a bar for those who wanted something different. Outside there were two bands playing, one by the swimming pool and one by the marquee and the buffet lunch, spread out on huge tables, was quite dazzling.

Feeling slightly overwhelmed by it all, John and I decided that the first thing we'd better do was cool down with a drink and since neither of us touches alcohol we had to make our excuses to the waiters and I went up to the bar for fruit juice.

'Two orange juices, please,' I said and as two glasses

tinkling with ice appeared on the bar a deep voice at my shoulder said, 'Are you on the wagon too?'

I looked round. It was Diana's husband, Alan Lake. 'No, it's just that we can't drink,' I explained. 'It doesn't agree with us.'

But Alan wasn't listening. He was staring at me as if he couldn't quite place the face. Then his frown disappeared.

'You're Doris Stokes, aren't you! I did enjoy your book. Do come and meet Diana.'

And that was how John and I became friends with Alan and Diana. We never did get around to visiting each other's homes, but we bumped into each other at functions and TV stations and when we heard that Di had cancer, the dreaded C as we called it, I rang her regularly.

Diana was a great fighter and at first it looked as if she'd won. As anyone who's had cancer knows, you have to keep going back for check-ups and no matter how healthy you feel, it's a worrying business. It can easily play on your mind and so to boost our morale at these difficult times, Diana and a couple of other friends and fellow sufferers, Julie Goodyear, the actress from Coronation Street, Pat Seed, who wrote the lovely book *One Day At A Time*, and I formed the Sod It Club. We used to get on the phone, have a good laugh and advise each other to say: 'Sod It! I'm not going to have it!' I don't know whether, medically speaking, laughter and defiance is the best way to react to the dreaded C, but it certainly made the four of us feel a lot better. In the nerve-racking days that surrounded the regular check-ups and tests those phone calls were like a tonic.

Diana seemed to blossom again. She went on a diet, exercised every day and swam in her pool and the pounds fell off. I bumped into her at TV AM one morning towards the end of her diet and I could hardly believe my eyes. Glamorous as ever, she was half her former size and she looked sensational.

'You make me want to spit!' I joked when I saw her

because we'd both been fighting a losing battle with our weight for months and now she put me to shame.

Diana laughed, delighted. 'You're never too old, Doris! You're always telling me that! You could do it too if you tried.'

'I never stop trying!' I wailed. 'And look where it gets me!'

They were a devoted couple, Alan and Di. They were always together. At parties and receptions they didn't split up and talk to people separately the way some couples do. They preferred to move round as a pair, Alan very dark and handsome with the cravat he always wore, and Di bubbly and full of fun, the silvery blonde hair bouncing when she laughed.

They'd had their problems, of course. Alan was an alcoholic and at the height of his illness he became very violent but Di stood by him.

'They always turn on the one they love,' she said and knowing that she stayed and helped him to beat his addiction. She was a very wise lady. Diana was the strong one in that partnership and, as the old saying goes, she really was his mother, lover, friend and wife. For his part, Alan worshipped her.

The last time I saw Di was at Robert Maxwell's. The annual reception had come round again and it was beginning to be a regular date in our diaries. There was no sign of the Lakes when we walked in this time, but as we loaded our plates at the buffet table they appeared.

Alan, charming as ever, was at my side in an instant to help me to the food.

'Caviar, darling?' he asked lifting a dish of what looked like miniature black ball-bearings.

'Oh no thank you, I don't like it,' I said.

He replaced the dish and tried another, 'Smoked salmon?'

'Oh no thank you, I don't like it,' I said again and at my other side Diana roared with laughter.

'It's no good, Alan. Doris and John only have cold chicken and a tomato!'

And I had to laugh because she was right. With all that rich food to choose from John and I invariably came away with just a bit of chicken and salad on our plates and possibly a bread roll to keep it company. The shame of it is that all this grand living has come too late for us. We'd never had the chance before to get used to caviar and smoked salmon and we're too old now to get started on that sort of thing. Apart from not liking the taste, we'd probably end up with dreadful indigestion!

Lunch was as merry as ever but for the first time I felt uneasy about Diana. She looked absolutely beautiful and yet something seemed to have happened to the figure she'd dieted so long to achieve. Her tummy looked enormous. Of course Diana enjoyed her food as much as the next woman but there was something about her shape that wasn't quite right. It didn't look as if she'd been on an eating spree, it seemed more serious than that.

As we moved away I said to John, 'There's something the matter with Di, I'm sure of it.'

Shortly afterwards we heard she'd gone into hospital with a stomach complaint. I was on tour at the time and dashing about from place to place with scarcely time to draw breath but between appointments I phoned the Lakes' home in Berkshire to find out where she was, and sent flowers to the hospital.

Then we were whirling off to the next town and by the time I caught up with the news, Diana was back home. Thank goodness, I thought to myself. It was a false alarm.

The weeks passed and then came the day I discovered I'd have to go into hospital again to have another lump removed. Of course I feared the worst the way you always do and I longed to talk to someone who'd understand. I didn't know if Diana was away or not but I rang her home on the off chance and she answered.

'Oh Diana, I'm so glad I caught you . . .' I said and soon I was pouring out all my troubles.

Diana was wonderful. She listened sympathetically to all my worries and when I'd finished she said, 'Oh sod it, kid. Just say you're not going to have it!'

And I couldn't help laughing. Thank goodness for the Sod It Club. And all the time I was moaning on to Di she knew that she herself was going to have to go back into hospital and the chances didn't look good – and she never said a word. What a wonderful lady.

My little operation was over quite quickly and I was up and on the road again when I picked up the paper one day and saw that Diana was back in hospital. I'd been feeling quite cheerful until that moment, but suddenly depression swept over me.

'Look at this, John,' I said pointing at the story, 'I think she's going to have a job to make it this time.'

There wasn't a moment to lose. I rang the hospital and after a short delay Alan came to the phone. They'd operated, he said but Di was too weak to talk at the moment. A cold feeling settled lower and lower in my stomach.

'We're thinking of you both, Alan, and praying for you,' I told him but as I put the receiver down I knew.

'I have an awful feeling about Di,' I told John, 'I don't think she's going to make it.'

A couple of days later we were having breakfast in our hotel room when the news came on the radio that Diana had passed. Even when you're expecting it the actual announcement is always a shock and my heart went out to poor Alan. I would miss Diana, of course, but I was relieved for her sake that it was over so quickly and she didn't have to suffer. She would be happy now with her family and her new life on the other side. It was Alan who needed help and sympathy. How was he going to manage without her, I wondered?

She had been his crutch in life. Would he find the strength to stand alone?

I can't honestly say that I was seriously afraid for Alan. I was worried about him of course and I felt desperately sorry for him but it didn't cross my mind that he might be suicidal. He and Diana were devoted to their fifteen-year-old son, Jason, and I never dreamed that Alan's despair would reach such a pitch that his need for Diana would over-ride his fatherly instincts. He was a good father and my first thought was thank goodness for Jason, he'll be the saving of his dad.

Not long after the announcement, Diana came through to me quite spontaneously, 'Tell Alan I'm only a whisper away,' she murmured in my ear, 'and that Minnie met me.'

Her voice was faint because she hadn't been over very long and it was difficult for her to communicate, but as always her concern for Alan was so great she felt she had to pass on some words of comfort.

I rang Alan immediately. There was a long pause. 'He's not taking any calls at the moment, he's too upset,' said the housekeeper, 'but seeing as it's you, Doris, I'll tell him you're on the line.'

The seconds ticked by and at last a distraught Alan came to the phone. 'Alan, I don't know what to say. There's nothing I can say to you,' I said gently, 'except, never forget, she's only a whisper away. I've spoken to her and she wanted you to know that Minnie met her.'

'Minnie's my mother,' he said brokenly, but he seemed relieved to know that Diana was all right and she hadn't been alone.

I didn't go to the funeral. I try to avoid conventional funerals whenever I can because spiritualists believe that a funeral should be, as far as possible, a happy occasion, when you celebrate the fact that the person who's passed on has taken his 'promotion' as we call it, and is free at last of all pain and suffering.

So I didn't go to the funeral but afterwards I phoned

Alan every week, on Sunday mornings when he came back from Mass, to give him what support I could. The months went by and my life became ever more hectic, yet somewhere at the back of my mind it registered that Alan wasn't recovering from his grief the way he should. He put on an act when he first picked up the phone, but good actor though he was you could tell. Then suddenly he'd break down and the phone would go dead.

To be honest I don't think anyone could have prevented the tragedy. A lot of Alan's friends blamed themselves for not realizing how ill he'd become and I felt guilty myself because the Sunday before it happened I hadn't phoned him. It was one of those things you regret for ever. I've already mentioned the bad back that plagued me that summer and by this stage it had reached such a pitch that the doctor decided to send me to hospital to have it looked at.

I was going in the next day and that Sunday I was in agony, but struggling to cook lunch, get my case packed and leave everything organized for John and Terry. All day I kept thinking I must ring Alan, I must ring Alan, but somehow I didn't get round to it. In hospital the next day it was the same. I'd taken the phone number with me and I fully intended to make the call but I was wheeled here, there and everywhere for tests. There were consultations with doctors, a stream of visitors and phone calls and all at once it was bedtime and I hadn't phoned Alan.

'Oh well, I'll definitely phone him tomorrow,' I said to myself. But Tuesday was the same.

Then on Wednesday, John switched on the television in my room just in case there was something on and then left it babbling to itself the way he often does. No one was taking much notice, when suddenly there came a news bulletin that stopped me in my tracks. Alan Lake had shot himself that morning at his Berkshire home.

I felt absolutely sick. If only I'd made that call –

perhaps things would have been different. Why hadn't I paid more attention to that nagging in my mind? It was so persistent I recognized it now as the spirit world's attempt to alert me to Alan's plight but I was so bogged down in my own problems I couldn't see it at the time. And what would happen to poor Jason? The more I thought of him the worse I felt. Poor boy to have lost both his parents so tragically and in such a short space of time.

It went round and round in my mind and by the end of the day I was in a right old tangle and inclined to blame myself. Fortunately, Ramanov came that night to talk some sense into me.

'Don't worry yourself, child, about things that can't be changed,' he said when I'd all but given up hope of getting to sleep. 'It is a waste of energy. There was nothing you could have done. It would have made no difference in the end, whether you made that phone call or not. Learn from this and go forward. Don't look back.'

And of course he was right, as I was to learn from Alan himself later.

It's strange how one chance meeting on a summer's day can lead to so many others. Just before Christmas I was invited by *Woman's Own* to their special Children of Courage service at Westminster Abbey and who should I bump into but Jason.

He was a beautiful child. Very like Diana but with light brown hair rather than blonde, yet when he moved you could see Alan in him.

After the service he came up to me and I noticed that his shirt collar was all frayed and I thought his mum would go mad if she saw it. But that's what kids are like. They have their favourite clothes and they won't stop wearing them.

'I'm going to America, Doris,' said Jason, 'what d'you think?' He had a stepbrother in America from an earlier marriage of Diana's.

'Well, love, you go,' I said, 'and see if you feel happy

71

living with Gary. But if you don't, come back because there are plenty of people here who'd like to give you a home.'

I was very impressed with Jason. The sadness was there at the back of his eyes but he was so brave and so mature you'd have thought he was nineteen rather than fifteen. He wasn't at all bitter against his father as some boys might have been.

'I was angry at first,' he admitted with that steady gaze so like Diana's, 'but I don't blame Dad now. He was hopeless without Mum.' And then he was a child again needing reassurance. 'They are still with me, aren't they, Doris?'

'They *are*,' I said firmly, 'and what's more your Mum in particular is watching over you and she's going to be helping you every step of the way.'

And suddenly over the hub-bub around us Diana's voice came chiming in. 'You'd better believe it.'

My contact with the Lake family didn't end when Jason went to America, however. Not long afterwards, to my amazement, I received a phone call from comedian Freddie Starr. Apparently Alan Lake had been his best friend and ever since the tragic suicide he'd been haunted by the feeling that Alan was trying to get in touch with him. Could I possibly help?

I looked through my diary doubtfully. It was booked up solid for months ahead. The only spaces occurred on Sundays, my day off. Now, as I've said, my Sundays off are precious to me. I can't do my job properly unless I have free time to recharge my batteries and of course I like some time at home with my family like everybody else.

Yet Alan and Diana were good friends to me. Diana in particular had always spared the time to listen and to cheer me up when I needed the support of the Sod It Club. If they were really trying to get through to Freddie and they needed my help then surely I owed it to them to see him. I picked up my pen.

'Well, Freddie,' I said, 'I'm afraid I only have Sundays free.'

'That's all right I can make Sundays,' said Freddie writing down the address. 'Now which garden can I land the helicopter in?'

I thought I was hearing things. 'Did you say helicopter?'

'Yes,' said Freddie, 'I was going to pop across in my helicopter.'

I laughed. 'Freddie, where d'you think I live? There's no room to land a helicopter in my pocket handkerchief garden. I'm afraid you'll have to come by car.'

But Freddie was so keen to set his mind at rest that the inconvenience didn't bother him. I'll let him explain for himself:

'Alan was my best friend and ever since he died I've had this feeling that he was still close to me. It was as if he'd left something unfinished between us and there was something he wanted to say to me. I had this feeling all the time but most strongly of all when I passed the graveyard where he was buried. It was like a magnet pulling me to the grave.

'Once I stopped the car at three o'clock in the morning and got out and went to the grave because it felt as if he was calling me. Yet no matter how hard I tried I couldn't hear what he was saying. It had been like that for months ever since the day he died, but after I found myself at the grave at three o'clock in the morning I knew I was going to have to do something.

'The next day I phoned Doris.'

Everyone thinks that Freddie Starr is just a zany comedian without a care in the world, but in fact he's a very sensitive, loving man. Just before he died Alan visited Freddie's home and when he left, he said goodbye and walked away through a garden gate. Freddie never saw him again and from that moment on he couldn't bear to look at that garden gate. It caused him so much pain that in the end he had it bricked up.

But, of course, before our first meeting I didn't know how nice Freddie was and I was a little apprehensive. I didn't know what to expect. Yet at four o'clock on that Sunday afternoon there was a knock at the door and in walked a compact, slimly built man with blond hair and the most beautiful blue eyes I've ever seen on a man. I've heard it said that some comedians are really very serious men and not at all funny off stage. Well I don't know whether that's true or not, but all I can say is that Freddie had us in stitches.

I didn't realize it then but he's a brilliant ventriloquist and hardly had he sat down when the bottles of drink we keep on the trolley for visitors began to talk. I glanced up in surprise and I distinctly heard a bottle of rum say:

'I don't need your ear, Doris, I'm a spirit!'

Well! It was definitely not a message from the other side, that was certain, but had I finally flipped as my mother always predicted? I looked round anxiously to see if the others had heard it too and then I noticed the mischief sparkling in Freddie's eyes.

'Freddie!' I gasped. 'It's you!'

'I'm a spirit, I'm a spirit!' insisted the rum while Freddie sat motionless, his lips not moving. But then he burst out laughing and gave the game away. Undaunted the other bottles started chattering too, and John and I laughed till we had to beg Freddie to stop because we were aching so much.

But of course Freddie had come for a sitting so the afternoon wasn't just confined to fun. There was work to be done too. Yet the work wasn't difficult because Alan was there immediately I tuned in. Freddie was right. Alan was anxious to talk to him. He wanted to explain to his old friend why he'd felt driven to take his own life and to reassure Freddie that nothing could have prevented it.

'It's Alan, darling!' he said straight away as soon as I began concentrating and his voice was as deep and rich as I remembered it. 'Tell Freddie about the black cravat. He was looking at the black cravat.'

I was puzzled but then I'm often puzzled by things the spirit people tell me so I just passed the message on to Freddie.

He looked blank at first but then he smiled. 'Last night I got Alan's photo album out and I was looking at a picture of me and Alan together,' he said. 'I noticed that Alan was wearing the black cravat that he wore all the time after Diana's death.'

'Well Alan must have been with you last night, love,' I said.

'Can he hear me now?' asked Freddie.

'Of course he can.'

'Right, Alan,' said Freddie to point over my shoulder. 'I was so mad at you for what you did. Did you know that? I was so bloody annoyed.'

'Look, Freddie, speak truthfully,' said Alan, 'if you'd been in the same boat and it had been Sandy you'd lost – could you have gone on?'

Tears sprang into Freddie's eyes and he looked at the floor. 'No, I don't think I could.'

'I hadn't planned to do it,' Alan went on, 'but I saw no future without Di. I never went back to the sauce (drink) but I'd started smoking again and I was so depressed.'

Then despite my protests he insisted on telling me what happened. Apparently out of the blue one morning he'd just decided he'd had enough. He didn't want to go on any longer. He just couldn't face it. He got his gun, rested the butt on the floor between his legs, leaned over, put the end of the barrel in his mouth and pulled the trigger.

'I felt a pain in my jaw, then blood came into my throat and that was it,' said Alan.

He told Freddie that since then the family Cadillac had been sold but the red car he used to drive was still there.

'We're together now,' he went on, 'but I got a

75

tongue-lashing from Diana when I first got here. She was furious about Jason.'

Then there was a weakening in the vibration and a woman's voice cut in. It was Diana.

'I was so angry,' she spluttered, 'I was livid. What was he thinking of leaving Jason like that? I told him he was a selfish bastard. After all I had no choice, but *he* did. But then I realized that Jason's probably better off this way. Alan's so weak he might have gone back on the drink and that would have been worse for Jason in the long run. Now at least he can remember his father as he was.'

And then she added, woman to woman, just the way she used to, 'I don't know. I'm still mothering him. I was mothering him then and I'm mothering him now, but mind, I love him.'

Other voices were crowding in now and I got an impression of a whole group of people jostling and eager to talk to Freddie.

'I'm Richard but everyone calls me Dick,' said a man loudly.

'That's my father,' said Freddie.

'Will you ask him to forgive me,' said Dick. 'He thought I didn't love him because I wasn't very demonstrative but I did. The trouble was I could never work out whether our Freddie was mental or whether he was a genius.'

Freddie laughed. 'Well I'll settle for half of that. I'm a mental genius!'

Dick went on to mention Jack, Freddie's stepfather and to say how pleased he was that Freddie's mother had married again and to tell her not to feel guilty about it because he wanted her to be happy. He also mentioned Muriel.

'That's my Auntie Muriel,' said Freddie in surprise, 'I've not seen Auntie Muriel for about twenty-five years.'

'Well Dick says that Muriel's been in hospital recently,' I said.

76

Freddie shook his head. 'I wouldn't know. I've not seen her for so long.'

But in fact Freddie checked with his mother the next day and it turned out that Auntie Muriel had had an operation only the month before to improve her hearing.

Dick also remarked that he enjoyed Freddie's shows and that he'd been with him to Barbados and to Canada.

'I hope he paid!' said Freddie.

Then, towards the end when the power was failing, Alan came back to say he was sorry for what he'd done and to thank Freddie for looking after Jason.

Afterwards, although it had been lovely to talk to Alan and Diana again, I felt drained. It had been an emotional sitting particularly since they were personal friends and Freddie seemed to sense my fatigue. He sat on the rug by the fire and talked quietly.

'What d'you think God is, Doris?' he asked suddenly.

It was a big question but he was quite sincere.

'Well I can't visualize God as a person,' I said. 'To me he is a divine power. That's the only way I can put it in words.'

Freddie was silent for a moment then he said. 'You know they spell it wrong. It shouldn't be G-O-D. It should be G-O-O-D because everything good is God.'

I thought that was beautiful.

In all Freddie stayed five hours. Although he arrived at four o'clock with the intention of staying half an hour or so, he didn't leave until nine o'clock at night. And being Freddie, the serious mood soon passed and it wasn't long before he had John and I in fits of laughter again. I don't think we've laughed so much in years. Freddie certainly did us more good than any medicine the doctor could prescribe.

As he was leaving, he put his arms round me and gave me a big hug.

'I'm going to give you a gift,' he said, blue eyes sparkling in that teasing way he has.

'Oh how lovely,' I said. I adore flowers and people often give me flowers after a sitting. Thanks to my sitters the house is always filled with the scent of fresh flowers.

'Yes,' Freddie went on, 'I'm going to give you a race horse.'

I nearly fell out of my chair, the placid response strangled somewhere in the back of my throat.

'A race horse?' I gasped half choking. 'Freddie, you're winding me up.'

'No I'm not,' said Freddie, his face going serious again. 'We've just had two foals born and I'd like to give you one. I'll keep it at my place for two years then you can choose your colours and put it with a trainer.'

I was overwhelmed and to tell the truth I couldn't believe he was serious. I mean whoever heard of an old lady in a London semi owning a race horse?

Yet Freddie meant it – as I discovered a few weeks later when he invited us over to see the foal.

It was a wet and windy Sunday morning, the sort of day when you look at the weather and wonder in a depressed way if spring is ever going to come. Yet for once the weather didn't bother me. I was as excited as a child on Christmas morning about meeting my foal. Although I must admit I was a little nervous too because I've always been a bit frightened of horses.

We splashed for miles through the dripping Berkshire lanes and at last turned in through a neat brick entrance. On either side all I could see were paddocks with horses and acres of lawn and trees. The drive seemed to go on for ever, and then suddenly there was a beautiful mansion in front of us and Freddie waving at the door.

He led us through into the hall and before I'd even unbuttoned my coat, two small blonde heads came charging towards me.

'Hello, Doris!' cried the little girl throwing her arms around me. This was Donna aged nine.

'Hello, Doris!' cried the little boy, Jodie aged five, doing the same.

They were lovely children. They'd just come back from a holiday in Spain so they had healthy brown faces and their father's bright blue eyes that shone even bluer against their tanned skin.

We sat down for a cup of tea, enlivened by Jodie's display of break dancing, then we all put on wellington boots and tramped up to the stables to meet my foal.

Jodie danced at my side as we squelched through the mud.

'I've got a horse too,' he told me, 'but not as big as yours, Doris.'

'Is my horse big?' I asked, alarmed. 'I thought it was only a baby.'

'Oh yes,' said Jodie. 'Bigger than mine.'

And in fact the horse *was* larger than I'd expected. When Freddie had said it was a foal, I'd imagined a tiny, fragile little creature staggering after its mother on matchstick legs, but the animal the groom led out into the stable yard was as tall as me. Nevertheless he was obviously very young, and nervous, and quite lovely. His coat was a beautiful reddish brown, he had a white diamond on his forehead and one white sock and when I stretched out my hand to stroke him, he put a nose into my palm that was as soft as velvet.

'Aren't you *lovely*!' I told him, 'I'm going to call you Stoksie.'

Freddie walked him round to calm him and then turned him loose into a paddock to play. He was a joy to watch. He galloped about revelling in the grass and the rain and kicking up his heels like a spring lamb.

'Freddie, he's the most beautiful gift,' I cried in delight. 'I love him.'

But the fun wasn't over. Freddie and his wife Sandy went to a great deal of trouble to give us a lovely day. I'd told Freddie not to bother about organizing a lunch.

'Sandy doesn't want to be working on a Sunday,' I said, 'a sandwich will do.'

79

But Sandy had laid out a delicious spread that included *vol-au-vents* and smoked salmon and must have involved as much work as a roast dinner.

Afterwards Freddie showed me the house. It was absolutely magnificent. The guest bedrooms alone were like hotel suites and one of them came complete with bed, bathroom, sofa, piano, TV and video. Freddie's own personal bathroom was all red and gold and columns and things like some impossibly luxurious picture in a glossy magazine, and his bedroom was lined in red pleated silk. I'd never seen anything like it. It really did take my breath away.

'You should have all this, the work you do, Doris,' said Freddie as he led me back downstairs again.

I shook my head. 'Freddie, it would scare me to death,' I told him and it would too. I'm grateful for my three-bedroom semi. I couldn't cope with a grand mansion.

Back in the sitting-room little Jodie was jumping about and exchanging meaningful glances with his father.

'Can we start now, Dad? Is it time?' he kept whispering.

Freddie evidently decided it was because we were requested to take seats and father and son disappeared to return a moment later with guitars. There they stood, father and son, Freddie with his guitar and beside him like a miniature replica, Jodie with his tiny guitar. Then Freddie started playing and singing and Jodie strummed away at one chord. Freddie went down on one knee and Jodie went down on one knee and all the time the little lad kept looking up at his father to check he was doing the right thing.

We all clapped heartily at the end of the performance, but Jodie hadn't finished yet. His tiny drum kit stood in the corner and when the applause died away there was an official announcement.

'Ladies and gentlemen, there will now be a cabaret in honour of Doris, performed by Jodie Starr.'

Grinning eagerly, Jodie bounded to his drums and gave us a very spirited rendering of something modern. I don't know what it was but it was very good and afterwards Jodie jumped down and gave a solemn bow and we all had to clap, then he ran off through the kitchen door and came back to take an encore. It was magic. Absolute magic.

We went home that evening, happy, full of food and convinced that the Starrs were one of the nicest, most unspoiled families you could wish to meet.

Chapter Six

At first there was nothing but a feeling of horror. Stark, terrifying, pure horror. Then a confused series of images. Bumping along in a car, then a dimly lit room and all the time the horror was growing until suddenly the impressions were shattered by a child's piercing scream. The pictures went blank and there was nothing but the terrible cry, 'I want my Mummy! I want my Mummy,' echoing round my head.

Cold and shaking, I lit a cigarette. A medium's job is not a cosy one. Every person who comes back to talk from the other side, describes the manner of their passing and not everyone is lucky enough to go gently in their sleep. I hear of illness and accidents, suicide and murder. I've spoken to young boys who've shot themselves and little children who've been stabbed to death, but nothing I've encountered so far, prepared me for the case of Lesley Anne Downey – one of the victims of the notorious Moors Murderers, Ian Brady and Myra Hindley.

No other case has left me with such a sick, cold feeling as if my tummy was filled up with ice. At the end of it I was mentally and physically exhausted and despite the central heating and the fire going full blast, it was hours before I felt really warm again.

I'd had no idea when I got up that morning, what I was letting myself in for. My diary said I had a sitting with a Mrs West who'd lost a child. Apparently a newspaper reporter had rung Laurie and asked if we could possibly see this lady because she was absolutely desperate. He gave us no other details and I was booked up for months ahead, but something told me it was important to see this mother. When the spirit world nudges me like that it's very unwise to ignore it so we did a bit of rearranging and juggling with dates and we made an appointment for Mrs West.

Just before she was due to arrive, I tuned in and immediately I heard the name Lesley, followed by a fleeting glimpse of a fragile, dark-haired little girl. A pretty little thing. Then the bell was ringing and I hurried out to the hall to open the front door.

Mrs West absolutely rushed in, there's no other way of describing it. She flew into the hall and gave me a big hug that spoke of years of pent up emotion.

'I can't believe it,' she said, 'I can't believe I'm actually here.'

You poor soul, I thought, my heart going out to her. You've been searching for a long time, and I prayed very hard that I'd be able to help.

She was an attractive woman was Anne West, with nice clothes, carefully blonded hair and beautiful eyes. Yet when you looked into those eyes you could see a great well of despair and emptiness. There was such a bleak quality to her unhappiness that I knew her daughter's passing had affected her very badly.

'Well come on in,' I said leading them into the sitting-room, 'and let's see what we can do.'

The reporter who'd brought Mrs West had a tape recorder and afterwards he very kindly gave me a transcript of the sitting. This is how it went:

DORIS: I can't promise you anything, my love. But I know you have come here with all this love in your heart and I only hope I can do something to help you. All I know is that your name is West and one of your little children passed over tragically. I started to tune in this morning and I got the name Lesley but her other name was not West.

MRS WEST: No, it was Downey. I married again.

DORIS: Where do I get the number ten from? Was it ten years ago when she passed?

MRS WEST: She was ten years old when she died.

DORIS: She will come back first as a child and later as the grown woman she is now. She tells me there's been four passings. She's telling me I'm not on my own because Mum has had other tragedies. Who's Terry?

MRS WEST: He's my son. My eldest son.

DORIS: She's talking to someone. I think it's Alice, Annie, Alan. She's telling me you haven't got it right, Doris. Listen. Yes, my love. It's Alan.

MRS WEST: Alan's my husband.

DORIS: She's talking about Alan. I thought she was talking to someone on the other side and she's told me to listen carefully. She's telling me he's very good to Mum. I love him for that. Who's Bill?

MRS WEST: My Dad.

DORIS: She's saying Bill's this side Doris. Try again love. Was that Millie. Molly. No it's Mary. Do you know a Mary on your side? No? We won't take it, love. We haven't got it right, love? Forgive me she's talking about Myra. She's saying don't upset yourself Mum over what you read in the papers about her being paroled. It's not going to happen because that woman will never reform. She's just play-acting. She's bad, Doris, really bad.

They were taking you where, love? They made you go with them? We were going for some fish and chips. Two of us went with them to show them where the chip shop was. We never went home again, Doris. Don't relive that, love. Your mum has had to live with this for years. Who is Vickie, love?

MRS WEST: My grand-daughter.

DORIS: Mum's got a red rose by my picture frame – thank you for that Mum. Alan thinks as much about me as my Mum, you know. Edward wants to say hello because no one ever talks to him. I'm ever so glad you came Mum because I wanted to tell you everything was all right.

I spend my time among the children Mum. The

children and the babies who have been taken back because no one wants them. But I love them and I spend all my time with them. I never had the chance to have babies of my own but I have lots of them to love here. Bill's here, Mum. And Jim wants to say hello.

MRS WEST: My brother.

DORIS: And Joe and Philip are here too.

MRS WEST: They're two old friends of mine. Brothers. They lived near us and died within two years of each other, about five years ago.

DORIS: She's grown into a beautiful girl, love. Auburn hair, or brown with touches of auburn. A beautiful woman. I have fulfilled my life, Mum. She's asking about a locket you wear with her picture in it.

MRS WEST: I usually wear it. I left it at home today.

DORIS: She's talking about Elsie.

MRS WEST: That's my sister.

DORIS: She's getting so excited and bubbling over. It's difficult love. John. He went over tragically. He should not have gone over.

MRS WEST: John was my nephew. He died three years after Lesley when a simple operation went wrong. They were devoted to each other.

DORIS: Are you all right, darling? Yes, I know it's difficult. No Lesley, you're talking to your Mum and I can't catch you. Mill Street?

MRS WEST: That's the police station where we first reported her missing. We went at four-thirty in the afternoon and they didn't want to know. Told us to go back later if she hadn't come home. It was ten-thirty before they started looking for her and there had been a fall of snow in between. That wrecked any chance they had of finding her.

DORIS: I met a man called Frank here. He used to be a policeman at Mill Street.

MRS WEST: Yes. Frank Rimmer. He was a sergeant.

DORIS: He helped when it happened to me and he is over now. I was able to say thank you to him for trying to help. He said he only wished they had been able to stop it. But they did try, Mum, didn't they?

I see my Mum a lot, Doris. I was listening when they were talking about going to Spain.

MRS WEST: We were trying to work out whether we could afford a holiday in Spain because Alan is about to lose his job. That was only two nights ago in the kitchen at home. We haven't even mentioned it to anyone else.

DORIS: I was listening, Doris. I was saying go on Mum and Dad. Do it. Life is too short to miss anything. Look how short mine was.

She's talking about a caravan holiday she really enjoyed.

MRS WEST: Yes. She went away with the Sunday school to Wales, three months before she died.

DORIS: Best holiday I ever had. I did have a good time then this had to happen. Now I'm grown up I realize you must get through to kids they must never go off with strangers, but you just don't think when you are a child. You trust everyone.

Don't go on with that love. It's only upsetting your Mum and you as well.

What are you laughing at, love? A pub? The Green Man? Tell them I was with them in the Green Man, Doris. With Alan and Tony.

MRS WEST: Tony is Alan's brother. We had a night out with them when we came from Manchester to London to visit them.

DORIS: Don't worry Alan. Everything will work out. I can see from this side. Live your life, Mum, you've suffered enough. Be happy and do the things you want to do. I'm okay. I'm happy. When we came we were in hospital. They nursed us back. I had a spirit Mum for a while until I grew up and grand-dad came. So don't worry that no one looked after me. I know you were afraid I was on my own but we are not. Nothing hurts spirit

86

children. They are innocent so they are loved and taken care of.

I wish you'd stop laughing, lovey. I'll shake them. She's talking about a baby called Emma Louise.

MRS WEST: I don't know anyone like that.

DORIS: She's probably not born yet. Auntie Mo.

MRS WEST: That's Alan's sister.

DORIS: Well the baby's connected with Auntie Mo. She's talking about a stone in a graveyard. It's shaped like an open book.

MRS WEST: It's a grave by Lesley's. The book is open and the message of remembrance is carved into its pages.

DORIS: I often go and look at it when Mum's having a little weep over my grave, Doris. That's where they buried my body but of course I'm not there. I had a terrific funeral, Doris. There were so many people there. Mum gave me a big heart of flowers and she put a single red rose in the grave. It's been such a long time, Mum, but I've always wanted to say thank you for that. You gave it to me with love, Mum, and I brought it back with love. Mum has a single red rose by my picture at home, Doris. It's lovely.

MRS WEST: Yes it's a silk rose in a tiny rose glass by her framed picture in the lounge.

DORIS: She's really cheeky you know. She's talking about divorces in the family. Three of them.

MRS WEST: I can only think of two.

DORIS: Lesley says don't forget your own, Mum. Don't forget that one.

Bill's coming back. He's trying to tell me something, he's saying just say Rutland Street, love, and she'll know what I mean.

MRS WEST: Rutland Street was round the corner from where we lived when I was a child. My dad, Bill, used to drink at a pub called Joe Daleys' there.

I pray every night, Doris, that Lesley will one day appear to me. But it hasn't happened yet.

DORIS: You're trying too hard, lovey. Relax. It might happen. She says Mum still sees me as I was at the end. Wipe this out of your mind, Mum. We were cleaned up in hospital.

She says she played with someone called Claire. She lived next door. She's grown up now and is married. I used to play with Claire all the time, Doris. If I had been playing with Claire when it happened I would not be here now.

DORIS: What's that love? M what? You really loved her.

MRS WEST: Muriel, a Sunday school teacher on the caravan holiday. I was talking to her at Lesley's funeral and it was only then that she told me right through the holiday Lesley couldn't wait to get back home. She kept telling Muriel she loved me and missed me.

DORIS: She's talking about a tape. Something about a tape. No not those awful tapes at the trial. I mean the one Mum wishes she had kept. The one with me singing on it which got lost.

MRS WEST: It was a tape Lesley's brother Terry made of her singing her favourite song – *Bobby's Girl*. We had a stereo record player with a tape deck and he made the recording. Then he asked me if he could swap the set for a guitar and he gave the tape recording away as well. It didn't mean much at the time. But two months later Lesley was dead. And that was the only recording we had of her voice. It has broken my heart ever since that we didn't keep it.

DORIS: She's talking about someone called Edward. Edward is here and he wants to say hello. Because no one ever talks to him. He wants to say thank you. No one visits him.

MRS WEST: It's Edward Evans, another victim of Brady and Hindley. He is buried only a few feet from Lesley. It looks as if his grave has not been touched since he was buried. We try to keep it tidy. Tidying the grass and keeping the weeds down.

Lesley also mentioned the name Lillian, which Anne West couldn't place but afterwards it came back to her.

MRS WEST: What she was talking about was the day she had her waist length hair cut when she was about eight. She came home and Alan told her she looked like a boy and he was going to call her George. Lesley came right back at him and told Alan, if you're going to call me George, I'm going to call you Lillian!

There were a few things that Lesley told me which I didn't repeat out loud during the sitting for fear of upsetting her mother but I discovered afterwards that Anne West knew of them already. Most disturbing of all was the fact that rats had eaten the child's body before it was found. Anne confirmed that this was true and that she'd not even had a complete body to identify.

The story was a nightmare in every way. It was back in the early sixties when an apparently harmless young couple named Ian Brady and Myra Hindley began to look for victims on the streets of Manchester. To their family and neighbours they were a quiet, devoted pair. They worked together, lived together and were always in each other's company. They didn't seem to have many friends and they weren't interested in noisy parties or going dancing like so many people. Instead they were content to drive about in Myra's little van making frequent trips to the moors. Great country lovers were Ian and Myra.

What nobody ever suspected was that Ian and Myra buried bodies on the moors and then went back to picnic on the graves.

Three children were murdered before they were caught, John Kilbride, aged 12, Lesley Anne Downey aged 10 and Edward Evans aged 17. John and Lesley were both buried on the moors and Edward would have probably ended up there too, had the murderers not been arrested before they had the chance to move his body. Who knows how many children would have died if Myra's brother-in-law hadn't called the police when they tried to persuade him to help them move Edward Evans' body.

Poor little Lesley had been so happy before it happened. The last her mother saw of her was when she skipped out the door on Boxing Day 1964 with her two younger brothers and three little friends from up the road, for a trip to the special Christmas fun fair round the corner.

By all accounts they had a wonderful time. In fact Lesley enjoyed herself so much that when it was time to go she couldn't tear herself away. She asked her friend Linda to take her little brothers home while she went back for one last look at the roundabouts.

Her family never saw her alive again.

The world has become a more violent place since the early sixties and these days child murders seem to be getting ever more common, yet people still recall the Moors Murders with particular horror.

It wasn't just that the children had been killed, but that they'd been tortured before they were killed and Lesley Anne Downey's suffering was recorded on tape, presumably for the evil couple's gruesome enjoyment later. During the trial of Brady and Hindley the tapes were played to an appalled courtroom and afterwards the judge said:

'None of us are likely to forget them for a very long time.'

The memory of those anguished cries will probably haunt the listeners for the rest of their lives.

I don't believe in harbouring bitterness but I must say that I could understand how Anne West felt, particularly over the rumours that Myra Hindley was coming up for parole and might even be released from prison soon. If Lesley had been my child I would have found it almost impossible to put Ramanov's tolerant principles into action.

'It's the hate that keeps me going,' said Anne West quietly and with deadly sincerity. 'I will live until Myra Hindley dies.'

Her words made me shudder involuntarily. I believed her . . .

Chapter Seven

If I close my eyes and concentrate I can hear the music now. Da da, da da da da da da ... The distinctive opening bars of *Sunday Night At The London Palladium*. Every Sunday the sound of that familiar tune brought us hurrying from whatever we were doing, to our places in front of the television for a night of glamour, big names and good old fashioned entertainment.

Like millions of other families we sat glued to the set as Bruce Forsyth, or Norman Vaughan or even later I think, Jimmy Tarbuck, introduced act after act and the glittering Tiller Girls, all long legs and flashing head-dresses, high kicked their way round the famous revolving stage.

Sunday Night At The London Palladium was the highlight of our week and for the stars who appeared, it was the highlight of their careers.

I've lost count of the number of hours we must have spent watching those old variety shows and all I can say is thank goodness I'm not a fortune teller. If one night I'd glanced up and seen myself standing on that stage I'd have thought I was going mad. The idea that one day I might appear at the London Palladium would have seemed totally impossible and also quite terrifying. It was about as likely as John and I moving into Buckingham Palace.

Yet unknown to me, the years were gradually winding me towards that stage. Without realizing where I was going, I slowly progressed from draughty church halls to larger assembly rooms, from tiny provincial theatres to larger theatres, until at last in 1984 I was asked if I'd consider appearing at the Palladium.

The *Palladium*! Well I nearly had kittens.

'Oh, Laurie, I don't know,' I said. The very thought

brought me out in a cold sweat. 'It's one of the most famous theatres in the world. I mean the Beatles have been on there and just about every other big name . . .'

I mean Lewisham Town Hall was one thing, but the London Palladium . . .

'But Doris you've done the Dominion in Tottenham Court Road,' said Laurie at his most persuasive. 'That was no bother. The Palladium's very similar.'

Not in my mind it wasn't. I thought of all those plush balconies, the red velvet, the Royal Box. No, the Palladium was quite paralysingly different.

'We'd never fill it Laurie,' I said, stalling.

He grinned. 'Well let's give it a try and see.'

At that point I didn't really believe I'd actually do it. Even when Laurie said everything was fixed for December 16th I just nodded and humoured him. I didn't think it would really happen. You've still got the tickets to sell, my lad, I thought to myself. And when you can't shift them we'll have to cancel and forget all about it.

The day the tickets went on sale I was still convinced we'd have to call the whole thing off – until Laurie phoned that is.

'Doris, it's fantastic!' he cried, sounding so elated I thought he'd won the football pools.

'What is it, Laurie?'

'I've just heard from the Palladium. The tickets have sold out in an hour and a half. They say it's a record!'

I stared at the receiver blankly. 'Are you sure someone's not pulling your leg, Laurie?'

'Positive. They've gone. Everyone of them's gone in an hour and a half.'

I should have been beside myself with excitement, of course, but all I could think of was 'Oh heavens – that means I've got to do it. I've really got to go on at the Palladium!'

As December 16th drew near I hovered between excitement and panic. I tried on all my dresses, bought a couple more and still I couldn't make up my mind which one to wear. Worse still, my hair was a mess, I decided, and my nails were breaking up all over the place. But the fuss over details was only to cover the real panic going on inside. I was intending to get up on stage at the Palladium, in front of a sell-out audience without an act, without a script, without the ability to sing, dance or act, without anything definite at all and I was going to stand there and hope for the best. From thin air I was hoping the means would come to entertain the audience for two hours. Now this surely was madness.

My mother had always said I'd end up in a mental home. Was she proving right at last? Had I finally flipped? Supposing nothing happened? Supposing when I tuned in all I heard was the sound of my own thoughts? How on earth would I cope with those tiers and tiers of blank faces growing more hostile by the minute?

It was enough to give you nightmares.

'Trust,' Ramanov told me over and over again. 'Trust.'

And I pushed the doubts very firmly to the back of my mind. After all wasn't this the same problem I faced every time I did a sitting or appeared in any theatre? Yet while I was busy not thinking terrible thoughts, small decisions suddenly became overwhelmingly difficult. I swished through my wardrobe for the umpteenth time. Now should it be the pink, the blue or maybe the turquoise . . . ?

At last on December 16th I was sitting in the wings in a pretty dress of soft peach, waiting to go on and trembling from head to foot.

John Avery, the manager, came past and smiled at me kindly. 'Don't be nervous, Doris,' he said, 'but then you wouldn't be a star if you weren't nervous. All the big stars that come here are just the same when they're waiting to go on.'

I wondered if Roy Castle could possibly feel as bad as I did. It was hard to believe. He always seems so relaxed when you see him on television. I was thinking of Roy because I'd been given his dressing-room. Six days a week he and Tommy Steele were appearing in *Singing in the Rain* and Sunday, their day off, I'd moved in. I hoped he didn't mind. I was very careful not to touch any of his things. There were good luck telegrams and cards all over the place and cuddly toy mascots and the dressing-room itself was beautiful. Lovely and warm, with soft carpets and the ceiling all draped in pleats like a dome. It was a far cry from the church halls where I started, where you changed into your dress in the toilet because the only room back stage was full of people drinking tea and gossiping.

I always try to relax quietly for a few minutes before I go on so that I can tune in and hopefully get a name or two to give me a start. So sitting there in Roy Castle's dressing-room I closed my eyes and concentrated. I was in luck. After a moment or two I heard a young boy's voice. He wasn't very old, no more than fourteen I'd have said.

'My mother's coming tonight,' he told me, 'her name's Rita.'

'And what's your name, lovey?' I asked him.

'I'm Stewart,' he said.

And that was it. But it was a start. Something to get my teeth into when I stood there in front of that audience.

Then all at once, the show had started. Tony Ortzen, the editor of *Psychic News*, had introduced me and I was walking out on to the stage at the Palladium. There were the tiers and tiers of balconies that I remembered from the television show, the chandeliers and the acres of red velvet and there on the stage, standing on a piece of carpet and flanked by flowers, were the chairs from the Royal Box. Nervous as I was, I couldn't help thinking goodness me, the Queen's probably sat in this as I sat down. It was a weird feeling.

I did my little gossip at the beginning, as I always do to relax people and reassure them that I'm just like them and I'm not going to swing from the lights or wave my arms about or do any of the peculiar things that people unfortunately associate with mediums. Then I told them how I'd tuned in earlier.

'I got a little boy called Stewart who's looking for his mother,' I said. 'She's called Rita, or it could be Anita. They both sound similar to me. Is there a Rita or Anita here with a little boy called Stewart?'

There was an expectant silence, which grew and grew and my stomach started turning somersaults. Surely I hadn't mucked up my very first message?

And then, just as I was getting seriously worried, a woman stood up and walked, half-stunned to the microphone.

'I'm Rita and my son was Stewart,' she said faintly. We were under way.

After the weeks of anxiety, the evening seemed to fly past for me. Stewart talked about his family and the milkman, Philip. He was fond of Philip because he used to help him on the milkround. He raised a laugh when he said that a baby would be born and to ask Philip about it, and a few tears when he described how he was killed in a cycling accident.

Then there were various friends and family members who came to talk to Margaret who worked with mentally handicapped children and had the potential to be a medium herself. There was the mother who was worried because her son and his girlfriend were happily expecting a baby but had no plans to get married. Another tragic mother who had been buried with her dead baby and wanted to reassure her orphaned children that she was with them still and wanted them to enjoy their Christmas. There was the son looking for his mother, Jane Jones, and the father who'd been sent over without his teeth in. And so it went on and on.

Once or twice there were a couple of loud, unexplained bangs and out in the audience a light blew out for no apparent reason and I remembered that the

Palladium is supposed to be haunted. The resident ghost didn't put in an appearance though and I had enough on my plate with all the spirit people who wanted to talk to the audience without trying to contact anyone else.

Then, suddenly it was all over. We handed out the flowers I like to give to people who've had messages, there were cameras going off all over the place and at last I could escape to the dressing-room for a long cup of tea.

It was only when I sat down that I realized how exhausted I was. My hair and my back were wet with sweat and I felt too drained even to talk. Up the corridor in Tommy Steele's dressing-room they were having a party but I couldn't face it. Making conversation with all those people no matter how nice they were was too much of an effort. All I wanted was to get home to bed and so John and I crept out to the car and left them all to it.

'Hey, don't forget this, love,' said John as I stole away.

I looked back. It was the large box the doorman had brought in during the evening. It was marked 'fragile' and had been handed in for me at the stage door earlier. I make a point though of never looking at letters left at the theatre before I go on, and I was too tired now even to be curious.

'Oh. No. Could you bring it love, I've got my dress to carry.'

John picked it up. 'It's heavy,' he said in surprise. 'I wonder what it is?'

Back home he could contain himself no longer. Before he'd even got his coat off he was out in the kitchen with the box, sawing through the string with a knife.

From the sitting-room where I'd collapsed into my armchair I heard a low whistle.

'You'd better look at this, girl.'

I groaned to myself. 'Can you bring it in here, John?'

There was a pause and then out he came with the most enormous birthday cake tied in yellow ribbon, decorated with yellow roses and piped with the words, 'Happy Birthday Doris.'

I was so touched that tears sprang into my eyes. It was from a boy called Pat and he'd made it himself. Apparently he'd read in one of my books how John and Terry are apt to forget my birthday, coming as it does right after Christmas and how the spirit world once left me a gold rose outlined on the wall to cheer me up. This year he wanted to make sure my birthday wouldn't be forgotten so he'd sent me my very own birthday cake.

What's more the spirit world had even arranged a Christmas present for me through that same kind young man. The Palladium evening had come right at the end of a three week tour around the country and on top of moving house. Now here I was a week before Christmas and feeling so tired I could hardly move. I'd rashly invited a few friends over for Christmas dinner a day early on Christmas Eve. It had seemed like a good idea at the time. I could get all the cooking over with on Christmas Eve and relax on Christmas Day with nothing to worry about but a cold buffet. But now I was having second thoughts. I hadn't so much as unpacked my dinner service yet. It was still stashed away in a crate somewhere and frankly I didn't feel up to anything more strenuous than opening a tin.

This problem was still bobbing around in my mind the next day when I rang Pat to thank him for the lovely cake. We chatted for quite a while, and then the conversation got round to Christmas. What was I having for Christmas this year Patrick wondered.

'D'you know, Pat, I'm too tired to care,' I said. 'What I'd really like is for some caterers to come and do the whole thing for me. That would be better than any present.'

'I'll do it,' said Pat immediately.

'But Pat you're not a caterer are you?' I asked. I'd assumed that cakes were some sort of hobby for him.

'No I'm a chef,' he said.

'Well look it's very sweet of you,' I said, 'but I wasn't serious. It was only wishful thinking. I haven't even got my dinner service unpacked yet or anything.'

'Don't worry,' said Pat, 'I'll bring mine. Now don't you bother. I'll see to everything.'

And he was as good as his word. On Christmas Eve he arrived with a dinner service, coffee service and silverware. He even brought a candelabra. Then he sent me off to put up my feet while he cooked the turkey, vegetables and Christmas pudding. The meal was delicious and afterwards Patrick cleared away, and washed the dishes. I didn't have to lift a finger. It was the best Christmas present I could have had.

But the Palladium connection didn't finish there. Not long after Christmas, Rita Broadfield, whose son Stewart had come through right at the beginning and started the evening off, came for a private sitting. This time she brought her husband with her.

'Quite honestly I've come because I was afraid for my wife,' he told me sternly and I could see that he was deeply suspicious about the whole thing. He was probably afraid his wife was going to be taken in by some sort of weirdo.

'That's alright love,' I said. 'There's nothing to be afraid of. Just send out your love to Stewart and we'll see what we can do.'

As before, Stewart came along as soon as I tuned in. This time I could see him standing in my sitting-room beside his parents. He was a tall boy with fair hair and a lively face. It turned out that he was 13 and not 14 as I'd first thought.

He told me more about the accident.

'There were four of us at first,' he said, 'then two went off and there were just the two of us left. I was going up the bypass and then bang . . . It was the back of my head got hit . . .'

99

He talked of the heart of flowers his parents had given him at the funeral, the extension they were building at home and even Wilson School – the school he'd attended before the accident.

Then, right at the end, just as we were finishing sitting and the power was at its lowest ebb, Rita Broadfield said sadly, 'He never mentioned his sister.'

Stewart was at her side in an instant.

'Does she mean Caroline? I wouldn't forget Caroline.'

And that did it for his father. The pent up emotion he'd been supressing since the previous August when the tragedy happened came spilling out and he cried.

'Doris, there's no way you could have known all that,' he said afterwards. 'It was marvellous.'

Appearing at the Palladium has got to be the peak of anyone's career and once the big day was over I thought things would die down. Strangely enough though the reverse seemed to happen. If anything the fuss went on building.

Extraordinary news came from my home town of Grantham where tickets had just gone on sale for a show in a hall built over the exact spot where I was born. One Wong Row which in Chinese means Fresh Fields. Apparently there was a bit of a riot. The queue went right round the leisure centre where I was appearing, so that the end met the beginning and there were minor dust-ups over the number of tickets some people were allowed to buy. To add insult to injury ticket touts walked up and down selling tickets for £10 and £15 each.

Ticket touts! I thought in amazement. Anyone would think it was a pop concert. Perplexed, I put it down to the fact that it was my home town and probably a lot of people were curious to see what had become of the local girl.

But even stranger news came from SAGB, The Belgrave Square headquarters of the Spiritualist Association of Great Britain. I still try to give demonstrations there as often as I can, just as I used to in the early days when I first came to London and this particular week I had a free evening. The day the tickets went on sale however I had a desperate phone call from the chairman Tom Johannson.

'Doris, I don't know what I'm going to do,' he said, the panic rising in his voice. 'They've been sleeping out all night in sleeping bags. There's a thousand turned up and I've only got room for 180 and they're blocking the pavements so much I've had the police here.'

When I eventually arrived the place was like a refugee camp. There were people packed into every tiny space. They were sitting on boxes in the aisle, they were crammed standing, along the back wall, they were even overflowing on to the platform at my feet.

It was a daunting prospect and not for the first time I felt vaguely frightened. 'What do they want from me?' I wondered anxiously. 'What are they expecting? I can't perform miracles.'

Nevertheless it was a happy evening. There were a lot of animals. We had a dog called Barnaby back, a cat called Doodie and another cat called Candy. I thought at first they were talking about a girl, but no. Candy turned out to be a cat!

I also got two Andrews that night. The first belonged to a family from Wisbech near Cambridge.

'I've got a young man called Andrew,' I explained, 'and he's something to do with the police.'

'Yes,' said his father, 'he was a policeman.'

Then another man stood up. 'Our son's Andrew too. We've got an Andrew.'

And before he'd finished speaking the other Andrew came in loud and clear and it turned out that he too had a connection with the police. His father was a policeman.

I was so pleased, because it turned out that the parents had come all the way from Cheshire. They'd

101

left home at two o'clock in the morning, arrived in London at four o'clock and joined the queue.

We were in the depths of a very bad winter at this time and I'd cut my touring down to the barest minimum. I didn't have to be idle though, just because the weather was awful. I was able to use the time to do some private sittings – children wherever possible – and soon the sad cases were pouring through my door again.

There was something about one particular letter asking for a sitting that worried me and I asked the couple to come along. I'm very glad I did because during the sitting their son Alan told me that his father's hobby was shooting and that in moments of despair they'd talked of committing suicide. The father intended to shoot his wife and then turn the gun on himself. Alan of course was horrified by this idea. He begged them to promise that they'd never ever consider it again.

'Tell them I'm alright. I'm happy and I'll be there to meet them when their time comes,' he said. 'But that's not yet. They mustn't bring themselves over. They've got their lives to lead.'

Afterwards Laurie who'd organized the meeting received a lovely letter from them with a beautiful cameo enclosed, as a gift for me.

'Doris really helped Alan and I so much in bringing our son back to us,' wrote his mother. 'It was unbelievable. He was speaking to us nearly all afternoon.'

There were many other similar stories. There was the boy who'd suffered from a blood disease. Twice he thought he'd beaten it and then it started up again. He was only seventeen but he hadn't lost his sense of humour.

'Tell Roger I've seen Sue and I think she's a bit of alright,' he told me with a roguish wink.

Roger was his brother and Sue was Roger's new girlfriend. He also knew that Roger was wearing his ring, that his parents had planted a rose bush on his grave and that the old man in the end bed of his ward, old Walter, had since passed over and they'd met on the other side.

Then there was the young soldier only nineteen years old who was killed in Germany when the army vehicle in which he was travelling rolled over.

'There were three of us,' he said in disgust. 'And I was the only one who passed over. We were going home. Only forty-eight hours stood between the accident and when I should have gone home.'

He'd been bitter at first he told me. He was engaged, looking forward to getting married and then this had to happen.

'I've settled down now,' he said, 'but I was angry at first. I thought why did it have to happen to me.'

Then there was Sarah, an air hostess who went down too deep when she was scuba diving. She came and stood beside her mother as we were talking and I saw that she was the most beautiful girl with long blonde hair turned under and huge eyes.

'Yes I was attractive and I knew it,' she said. 'It was my own bloody fault. I was always a dare devil. I always had to go one better than anyone else.'

She struggled to give me an impression of what happened. Suddenly there was water all around me and she was putting something over my nose. I got an impression of swimming around looking at things, then there was a booming sound in my ears and nothing more.

'Yes she came to the surface too quickly and was incoherent,' said her mother. 'She was trying to pull off her mask. Her friend tried to pull her to the boat but she was too heavy and she was drowning him. He let her go and she slipped off the reef.'

But Sarah too could still laugh at herself.

'I'd just had all my dental work done. I had all my teeth crowned. If I'd known this was going to happen I'd have saved my money. It cost me a bomb!'

Afterwards Sarah's mother confessed that she'd been living with the fear of losing a child for a long time.

'I've always known I was going to lose one of them,' she said. 'I kept thinking it was a wicked thing to think but somehow I just knew. And I thought if it had to happen, let it be quick.'

Well it had been very quick. Sarah was enjoying herself, then suddenly she lost consciousness and knew nothing more about it until she woke up on the other side. That was one small comfort I could offer her poor mother. Sarah didn't suffer at all.

After sittings like these it's difficult not to feel sad. When you meet the grieving parents and speak to the young people, lovely children every one, it's hard not to feel a sense of waste. Yet I know that young as they are, they've done their time on earth and now they are happy and fulfilled in new lives on the other side.

We shouldn't weep for them because nothing can hurt them now.

Chapter Eight

They were making a valiant effort at the estate agents'. There was a big board nailed over the window and the neat rows of photographs of houses for sale had been taken down, but the name of the shop was still boldly outlined over the top and inside it was business as usual.

Set in a comfortable, suburban area amongst news-agents and grocery shops you'd have thought that the owner, doing particularly well, was simply having the place smartened up. In fact this ordinary looking estate agents, apparently no different from any other, was reputed to be haunted.

A number of disturbing events had worried the staff and the strange goings on had already attracted the attention of the local paper.

From what I could make out, there had been a series of unusual accidents, interspersed by small, but inexplicable incidents. First, during a spell when the electricity supply was off, workmen had come to install mobile gas heaters, and in a freak accident, one of the gas cylinders blew up, injuring one of the men. Not long afterwards a water pipe burst, flooding the shop and no sooner had they got the place dry than there was a terrible commotion outside and a car careered across the road, mounted the pavement and crashed straight through the estate agents window, missing the owner by inches.

As if this wasn't bad enough, less dramatic but equally worrying things were happening almost every day. There was a room at the back of the shop where there was a definite atmosphere – almost as if an unseen presence was watching and a dog belonging to one of the staff refused point blank to enter this room.

One day the owner was sitting there attempting to work when the strange atmosphere suddenly built up around her. She ignored it for as long as she could but in the end it became so oppressive that she had to run out of the room and slam the door behind her. So shaken was she by the experience that she couldn't bring herself to cross the threshold again until the next day.

In the outer shop objects were frequently moved about, the closed sign on the front door was often mysteriously turned around to read 'Open' when the shop was shut and one morning the staff walked in to find a house brick in the middle of the floor. It had not been there when they'd locked up the night before, no one else had been in the shop and there was no sign of forced entry and yet, somehow, the brick had found its way into the centre of the carpet.

It was the sort of story that papers love to print and readers love to read but not nearly so fascinating for the people involved. By the time the Thames News picked it up and decided it might make an amusing little item for the tea time show, the people in the shop were beginning to feel desperate. Most of all they wanted to know what was going on.

The first I heard of it was at 2.00 one afternoon when Thames News rang to ask if I could do an urgent job for them.

'Well when did you have in mind?' I asked uncertainly. The photographer from the publishers' had arrived and we were in the middle of doing the pictures for the cover of my new book.

'Straight away,' they said. 'We'll send a car for you.'

'I'm sorry but I don't think I can.' I explained, 'I've got the photographer here and we're doing a photo session.'

There was a hurried exchange at the other end of the phone, then the researcher came back. 'How long will you be?'

'I don't know, just a minute I'll ask.' I put my hand

over the mouthpiece, 'How much longer will it take?' I called out to the photographer.

It had already taken longer than I'd thought because I'd had to change. I'd worked so hard to make myself look nice. I'd put on a new navy blue dress with spots, navy blue stockings and navy blue shoes and I thought I looked marvellous, a real thoroughly modern Millie. And the first thing the photographer said when I opened the door was, 'Oh. Haven't you got anything lighter?'

So we trouped upstairs and looked through my wardrobe and he picked out an old pink dress that I've worn dozens of times before! So much for thoroughly modern Millie!

Anyway, by the time I'd changed and tidied my hair again we could have taken a whole roll of film.

Fortunately the photographer was a good-natured man and he didn't mind being rushed. 'Seeing as it's you Doris we'll get it done in an hour,' he promised.

I told the television people to collect us just after three o'clock and we galloped through the picture, then I dashed upstairs to change again, because the photographer had put me in a long dress and the viewers might think it strange to see me gallivanting round an estate agents' in evening dress at tea-time.

By now I was feeling distinctly breathless. What I didn't realize was that the peculiar jinx affecting the estate agents had now extended to include the TV story as well. And if you think jinx is too strong a word for it look what happened.

First of all, the driver the company used happened to be at home in Essex when the call came through and it took him some time to reach us. By the time he arrived the rush hour traffic was building up and ahead of us was one of the worst journeys you can make in London. I live in South East London and the shop was in North West London and separating us was a whole city of jammed, exhaust-fogged streets where the cars crawled at walking pace. Not surprisingly the journey seemed to last hours and by the time we arrived, the producer was getting rather anxious about his chances of finishing in time for the programme that evening.

'I don't like to rush you Doris,' he said, 'but we really do need to start filming at once.'

'That's alright love. You start and I'll do my best.'

But the cameras had hardly started rolling, when they stopped again.

'Sorry, Doris. The batteries have gone down on the sound.'

We took a break while the batteries were changed then we were off again, but a few minutes later the same thing happened. By now the producer was quietly distraught. The situation was practically unheard of he told me as he hurried off to phone the studios and get fresh batteries sent out by messenger.

In all three lots of batteries went down before we managed to start filming and then the crew announced that they finished at 6.30 and they were going home. I thought the poor producer would have a stroke but instead he looked resigned.

'Well we've no chance of catching the news now,' he said. 'There's no point in panicking.'

We sat down to wait for the new crew to arrive but when they turned up, our driver, who had been hanging around throughout all the disasters, suddenly told us that he had a date and he couldn't wait any longer. He was off. He climbed into his car, accelerated away up the road and that was the last we saw of him. John and I looked at each other and burst out laughing. You had to see the funny side or you'd go mad.

Fortunately the sitting went better than the filming. When we'd first arrived the owner took me into the room where the atmosphere was sometimes oppressive. She believed the trouble stemmed from this room and I felt she was probably right. I walked carefully round, checking for a presence. This must look rather strange to people who don't realize what I'm doing but in fact you can tell if there's an entity present by the cold spot. This is a place in an otherwise warm room which is freezing cold for no apparent reason. It's a strange sort of cold which creeps up from the floor and chills you to the bone. Once you've felt it, you'd never mistake a cold spot for an ordinary draught again. The sensation is quite different.

Well I walked around, pacing every bit of that room and nothing happened. The warmth was uniformly spread over the floor.

'He's not here at the moment,' I said at last, but as things turned out we had plenty of time.

When filming eventually started I went back to the room and this time I felt it straight away. Walking past the desk a stream of icy air suddenly flowed up from the floor freezing my right side. I stopped and as I did so the room shifted, swung before my eyes and somehow rearranged itself. The desk was different. I saw a dictaphone, two telephones and an in tray on the top and beside it a big swivel chair.

'This is how it used to be when it was my office,' said a man's voice.

The image held for a moment longer, then it disolved and I was back with the camera crew. I described what I'd seen and the new owner gasped.

'That's right. We've got a photo of it like that,' she said.

We were in business. The man wanted to talk. Apparently he'd run the estate agents some years before and got himself in a bit of a mess. Eventually he'd taken his own life.

'I went into the garage and did it in the car,' he said.

Now his main concern was for his wife. He hadn't been married very long and he wanted his wife to know how sorry he was for the misery he'd caused.

'There were two children,' he said, 'my wife had one and I had one. I'm afraid I treated her quite badly because I was worried.'

He had been moving things about at the shop he

admitted because he was trying to attract attention. He wanted to warn the new owner about a possible business problem and most of all he wanted a message passed on to his wife. Could they buy her some flowers as a token of his love and tell her he was sorry?

As further proof that he really had been one of the previous owners of the shop, he told me that he used to keep the keys in a very unusual place.

'I'll say,' said the new owner, 'he kept them behind the radiator.'

The one thing he wouldn't do, however, was claim responsibility for the accidents that plagued the shop. They were simply accidents, he insisted, and the fact there had been so many was unfortunate coincidence.

'And as for the last one, the car coming through the window, I'll tell you what happened there. The woman was pulling into the side of the road, went to put her foot on the brake and hit the accelerator instead. She lost control of the car and it shot across the pavement straight through the window. But don't let them blame me. I wouldn't do a thing like that. Someone could have been killed.'

By the end of our chat the man seemed much happier. We promised that the message would go to his wife and he said he'd leave the shop in peace.

At last filming finished. We'd long ago missed the early evening news but the producer said they'd keep the story and use it another night. It had been a very long day. By the time we got home it was nine o'clock and I hadn't even started the dinner. I just hoped I'd been of some help at the estate agents because a medium can't always put a stop to such 'hauntings'. I can't force a spirit person to do something against his will. I can only find out what's troubling him, attempt to put it right and endeavour to persuade him that it's time he accepted that his earth life is over and it's time he moved on to higher things. But spirit people don't have to take my advice any more than people here do.

People have some very funny ideas about 'ghosts'

and 'hauntings'. In fact 'ghosts' never 'haunt' a place in order to scare people – or at least I've never come across one like that. They tend to cling to places they have known either because they refuse to accept that their earth life is finished, or because they are desperately trying to communicate with someone and can't rest until they've done so. They very seldom drift about for nothing.

One of the most extraordinary and poignant 'hauntings' I've come across in recent years was brought to my attention by journalist Michael Hellicar. He had written an article about life after death for the *Daily Mirror* and afterwards one of his readers rung him in desperation. This poor man thought he was going mad because he kept seeing his wife who'd died only a few days before. Michael phoned me and asked if I could help save his sanity.

Well I did a sitting and I remember I picked up the wife very easily because she was hovering so close to her distraught husband. It seemed to go well but as far as I was concerned there was nothing particularly remarkable about the case. It was a tragic affair, but sadly I seem to hear so many similar stories these days. It wasn't until long afterwards that I heard the whole story from Michael Hellicar and then I realized I'd been involved in something very unusual indeed. I'll let Michael explain it to you the way he explained it to me.

Michael Hellicar: 'I had quite a big response to my story on life after death but the strangest of all was a phone call from a man whose wife had committed suicide the week before by jumping off a tower block near their home. Apparently her death wasn't entirely unexpected because she'd had a history of mental illness, but she was only twenty-seven, had left a young family and he was very upset.

'The reason he was phoning me was that he feared he was going mad. Apparently after he'd talked to the police, identified the body and gone through all the gruesome formalities, he went home, walked into the bathroom and there she was. Solid and real wearing the dress he liked her in and her usual perfume. He reached out and touched her and his hand didn't go straight through. Her flesh was warm and real and what's more she talked to him. She said how sorry she was for what she'd done, but that she couldn't explain why she'd done it. Then she went on to give him advice about how to bring up the children.

'The man was totally confused. His senses told him one thing and his mind told him it wasn't possible. Could this really have happened, or was he mad?

'Now I must admit at this point I thought he'd been temporarily deranged by grief. But I've been a journalist for 30 years and by now I can tell whether I'm talking to a crank or not. The peculiar thing was that this man seemed completely sane. What's more as he continued his story, it became stranger and yet oddly more plausible.

'The next day he'd woken convinced that he'd dreamed the whole thing and that grief had made the dream particularly vivid. He put it out of his mind and set out to break the news to his family. On the way though, he bumped into a neighbour and stopped to tell her that his wife had died the morning before.

' "Oh no," said the neighbour when she'd got over the shock, "it couldn't have been the morning. You must be mistaken. I saw her at the window yesterday afternoon watching for you to come home the way she always did."

'Puzzled the man assured her that his wife had definitely died in the morning. Later at his parents' home he was sitting at the table breaking the dreadful news when he saw his younger brother pass the window. His brother waved and a few minutes afterwards put his head round the door.

' "Hello," he said. "Where's Jan?"

'Everybody winced and the parents gently told him that Jan was dead.

112

Win Webb and Flo Hodson with my mum (far right)

Meeting Stoksie with Freddie

The wonderful poster for my tour

The first Christmas in our lovely new home

Happiness and tears after contact

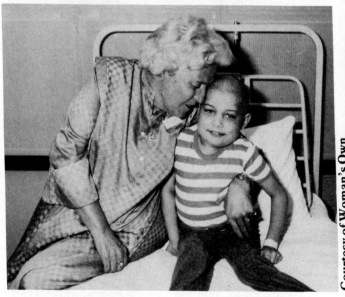

A proud moment. Princess Anne opens the Westminster Children's Hospital Bone Marrow Transplant Unit. Here with the Princess are Pauline and Brendan McAleese who lost their son, David, to bone marrow disease.

Cuddling lovely little transplant patient Matthew Hardy

SIDNEY VAUNCEZ meets Doris Stokes
She doesn't sing or dance, do tricks or tell fortunes but on stage . . .

SHE'S MAGIC!

Doris Stokes at Lewisham Theatre. (Picture Jim Selby)

"I THINK your name should live for ever," Freddie Starr told her, "let me give you something."

"That's not necessary, Freddie love" Doris Stokes replied. "I'm just happy I was able to help."

"No," he insisted. "I must let you have a gift. I know – I'll give you a racehorse!"

And so he did. It's a yearling named, after some discussion, Stokey and currently housed at Freddie Starr's stables.

Freddie, distressed by the suicide of his close friend Alan Lake after the death of Alan's wife Diana Dors, was inconsolable until a journalist acquaintance advised him to seek a sitting with Doris Stokes. What she told him after conversing in his presence with long-dead Diana and Alan gave Freddie comfort, peace of mind and the abiding conviction that she was the most wonderful person in the world.

Doris Stokes is a permanently cheery 65-year-old spiritualist. She's grey-haired, grey-eyed, a 13½ stone dumpling. Her weight, she says, goes up and down like a yo-yo because of thyroid trouble – not to mention a mass of other medical problems that beset her, including cancer. Yet despite her chronic ailments and not all that glamorous appearance, Doris is the world's most acclaimed medium. She isn't clairvoyant, that's to say she doesn't – except very rarely – see any of the dear departed, she's clairaudient. Like Joan of Arc she hears voices. The dead speak to her and she talks back in the matey-est

of terms with occasional prompting from her spirit guide, a Tibetan named – as near as she can spell it – Ramanov.

This sweet, elderly lady, who only needs a floral pinny round her tummy to look like the archetypal amiable suburban grandma, could earn as much per annum as Freddie Starr himself, probably the highest paid artist in Britain. She doesn't rake in that much because, unlike the hyper-energetic eight or nine shows a week Freddie, her health allows Doris to appear twice, or at most only three times a week, but the mere posting of Doris's name over a marquee can fill a theatre faster than most pop stars.

Last year, the packed London's huge Dominion Theatre solid for three successive nights. This summer she is taking over the Palladium for a series of Sunday evenings. The first three dates to be announced were July 14, August 4 and September 1 – but don't apply for tickers, they went ages ago. Her first London Palladium appearance last year likewise sold out in less than two hours.

There can't be a more modest theatrical presentation than her's. After a brief introduction Doris sits in an easy chair with the stage to herself and her voices. She simply oozes affection as she dispenses love and solace to everyone in the world's – this one and the next, for she recognises no line of demarcation. To Doris there is no death. As a survival medium she is convinced that the world of the spirits, is merely a continuation of ours. When she speaks of her many

friends in show business who have passed over like Dick Emery, Alan Lake or Diana Dors, it's always Dick-"is", Diana "is". Never "was". The past tense doesn't exist for her in this connection.

Doris doesn't pretend to be anything other than an old lady, maybe specially gifted as well, who plucks voices out of the air talking to them as friends about neighbours who identify themselves by disclosing how much one woman paid over the odds for a new gas stove, or why another hid her blue hat on top of the wardrobe. Hardly world-shattering revelations, but to a crowded standing-room only house itching for the slightest sign of contact with departed loved ones, they become riveting dramas in which they are themselves intimately involved. No fancy talk. No tricks, no illusions, no ectoplasm, no make-up or costumes. No telling fortunes. The dialogues with unseen dead proponents might appear to sceptics to be largely imaginary, but unquestionably even for them Doris Stokes, alive on stage is real magic.

She can't understand why everyone makes so much fuss over her. Why she was flown recently on a special plane to Australia for a jam-packed appearance at Sydney's prestigious Opera House.

"The dressing room there was bigger than my whole flat in South London," she confided to me. Dismissing this unwarranted luxury she continued: "Though my books sell very well, and my appearances make money, much of it goes in taxes and donations to charities. What do I want lots of money for, anyway? I've got my husband, John, my son Terry and my spirit family over there waiting for me – with probably not so long to wait either," she added with a genuine chuckle. "After all, I'm only a simple old country woman."

She's about as simple and uncomplicated as that other country woman, Margaret Thatcher whose parents ran a grocers shop across the way from the Stokes in Grantham.

"We didn't have much to do with them," Doris recalled, "or rather they with us. We Stokes were very poor and they were the 'snobby Roberts'. Her father was a lay preacher. Methodist, I think. Very strict. My father was a Romany, the first of his tribe to quit wandering and settle down in a permanent home. My mother and the rest of us were Church of England. I used to get a ha'penny from the Methodist elders to attend Sunday Services in their Chapel. I would clutch the coin as my hot little hand and listen to sermons about hell fire and damnation wishing all the time I could rush into the street and spend it on gob-stoppers.

"As for Margaret, quite a few years younger than me, she was a proper little madam. Never went out scrimping in the orchards with the other kids her age. Always immaculately dressed. Never a stain on her pressed school uniform. Not a bit out of place. Come to think of it" – with another guffaw – "she hasn't changed much!"

The robust speech and good humour of ordinary working folk has never deserted Doris. She is not above telling

some obstreperous other-world sprite in public not to be a silly sod and stop shoving. She may even start off sessions with jokes like the two mediums who meet by chance at Tesco's where one tells the other: "You're all right. How am I doing?" Or the story about the fitness fanatic who asks if they have any sports up there and is told to come back a week later when he is greeted with good news and bad news. The good is that they play cricket and football. The bad is that he will be captain on Sunday.

Danny La Rue is another great friend of the Stokes family. When both Doris and Danny were in Birmingham appearing at different theatres, they regularly visited each other's dressing rooms between shows. On one such occasion an enterprising photographer asked to take a picture of the famous pair together. Doris at first, refused. Although without a trace of vanity, she didn't want to be photographed in day clothes since a recent mastectomy had removed one of her breasts and she felt she looked a little lop-sided without its temporary replacement.

"I told Danny about my missing boob", she recounted without affectation. "I thought for a moment he'd say – I'll lend you one of mine. But he posed me carefully behind a large vase of flowers, called in the photographer and all was well."

On another mutual date in Birmingham Doris was in the audience with some friends when she noticed Danny's long-time manager Jack Hanson waiting in the wings. He wasn't backstage however and when she mentioned it to Danny, he told her Jack had just died in hospital. This was one of those rare moments when Doris was truly clairvoyant. Usually it's only voices, with the single visual indication of something or someone from another world present in the audience in the form of a light burning, strongly for a person who has passed over a long time ago, and faint and flickering for a recent bereavement.

Doris's voices never let her down. Before an evening session she spends the whole afternoon tuning into the spirit world, praying desperately that her voices will come through. They always do. Sometimes the voices she conjures up on stage will describe ordinary events that can build up into high drama. At the Dominion she asked a woman: "Have you still got that blue hat and matching gloves?" The answer – "Yes!" "I see the bag is still behind the wardrobe" – "Yes! Yes!" "She's met Ted after all" – "Yes!" "In Australia" – "Yes! Yes!"

"They've been together all the time. Didn't cost them a penny" – "Yes! – Yes!–Yes!" The tension rose like Molly Bloom's randy Ulysses monologue to culminate in a great orgasmic affirmation.

Doris receives more than 1,000 letters every week, each of her four books have been best sellers and she is constantly in demand for TV and radio shows. She has recently recorded an album on the LIPP label which has introductory music by the famous guitarist Bert Weedon, and contains a poem recited by Doris and dedicated to her dead son, John Michael.

The Palladium!

' "Don't be silly," he said, "I just saw her sitting with you when I looked through the window," and he described the dress she was wearing. It was the dress she'd been wearing in the bathroom the night before.

'More confused than ever the husband went home to find his wife's perfume filled the house and the dog refused to go upstairs. He walked into the bathroom and there she was again. This time she begged him not to brood about why she'd done it but to get on with his life and marry again.

'Shortly afterwards the phone rang. It was his in-laws. "You won't believe this," they said, "but we saw Jan last night. She came to the house and sort of melted through the wall."

'It was at this stage the man phoned me. After reading my article he thought I must be an expert on such things. Was he going out of his mind he wanted to know, and if he wasn't, what had happened to his wife? He didn't like to think of her just floating around.

'Well I met him and I was very impressed by how straightforward and normal he seemed. His story was incredible but he didn't seem to be unbalanced or lying. The only problem was that I couldn't answer his questions and I felt that if the situation went on much longer he'd have a breakdown under the strain. In the end I phoned Doris and asked if she could help. I didn't give her all the details. I just told her this man had lost his wife and thought he'd seen her after her death . . .'

Well, although I hadn't heard this extraordinary story it was quite obvious that this man's wife was anxious to talk to him. She was there the moment I tuned in and she told me her name was Jan and that she'd jumped off a roof.

'He's quite right when he feels that I'm close to him,' she said. 'Last night he was very clumsy and broke a teapot and today he went out and bought another one. It's a pretty yellow one. I like it.'

The astonished husband agreed that this was quite true.

Jan went on to say that she felt better now than she had when she'd first gone over. She was still full of guilt for leaving her family but she felt easier in her mind.

'At first I didn't want to tell him why I did it. I didn't want to cause trouble,' she said, 'but now I know that he needs to know and he won't rest until he finds out.'

And she went on to explain that there'd been a row with her mother and sister. Apparently in the heat of the moment they'd told her that she wasn't bringing up her children properly because she was always in and out of mental hospitals.

'They'd be better off without you,' they'd said. And Jan, in her disturbed state, promptly went out the next day and threw herself off a roof.

'But please don't blame them,' she begged her husband. 'It wasn't their fault. I was sick in the mind. I would have done it sooner or later anyway.'

She gave a great many family names, thanked her husband for removing the ear-rings in which she died and replacing them with her favourite pair and finally she mentioned a little surprise she'd been planning.

'I'd saved £15 to take the kids out to the seaside for a treat,' she said, 'it's hidden under a pillow in the cupboard over the wardrobe. Please give them a good day with my love.'

The husband promised that if he found the money he would. By now the power was growing weak. Few people realize that it's as difficult and tiring for spirit people to contact a medium as it is for a medium to contact them, especially when the spirit person has not long passed over. Jan was getting very tired and her voice faded.

'Tell him not to feel guilty if he meets someone else,' she said. 'I want him to be happy,' and then she was gone.

The sitting was over. Michael and the husband

stayed on a little longer, drinking coffee and I was pleased to see that the man looked much happier.

'So I'm not going mad, Doris,' he said, 'I really did see her?'

'I'm sure you did love,' I answered him, 'She's very close to you. It's only her old overcoat in that coffin.'

And of course it's not unusual for people to see loved ones who've passed over. It depends how psychic they are and how hard they are trying. Children are more psychic than adults and they see spirit people much more frequently but either they don't say anything for fear of ridicule or their parents don't believe them. As for adults I'm sure it's no coincidence that we see spirit people when we least expect it. Time and time again bereaved mothers or widows will tell me they keep trying to see their husband or child but nothing happens. I can only conclude that it doesn't work when you try too hard. Perhaps your conscious mind swamps the psychic part and drowns any psychic messages struggling to get through. I know that when I'm trying desperately hard to do well at my work I've often been disappointed with the results and yet at other times when my mind's not fully on it for some reason, if I'm not feeling too good or I'm thinking about something else – I've been astonished how clearly the messages have come through.

Anyway, Michael Hellicar and his reader eventually left and that was the last I thought of the matter. Michael Hellicar however, had become very interested in the case. He gave the husband a lift home and out of curiosity went inside with the man to see if the message I'd given them about the money hidden in the wardrobe was correct.

'We went into the bedroom and I saw that there was a bridging unit between two wardrobes,' Michael told me. 'The husband opened the unit and inside was a pillow. He lifted the pillow and underneath was £15 just as you told him. It was amazing.

'But that wasn't quite the end of the story. A couple

115

of weeks later I rang him again to see if the sitting had done the trick. He sound much better.

'Apparently after the sitting he'd found a note in his wife's handwriting on the dressing-table, yet it had not been there before. It read: "I'm sorry but now at least you understand." And since then she'd not been back and the dog was quite happy to go upstairs again.

'I'm quite happy now,' he said. 'I know my wife's alright and that she wants me to get on with my life.'

And as far as we know, that's exactly what he did.

Chapter Nine

'Doris,' said the woman at the microphone, 'can you help me?'

It was question time at Fairfield Halls, Croydon and she'd been patiently waiting her turn in the queue. A fragile little woman but she held her head high and she spoke out bravely.

'I'm living in agony because I know I'm not long for this world. I'm not frightened of death but I'm frightened of waiting for it,' she paused and swallowed hard. 'And . . . and I don't want to leave my family behind.'

My heart went out to her. Poor woman. She had cancer, of that I was sure and I knew how she must be suffering. I've been there myself. I've been lucky so far but I've had a glimpse of what it must be like for those poor souls who can't be helped by modern medicine. What could I say, in just a few moments, to comfort her?

'Well, darling,' I said gently, 'you can't take your family with you, can you? But remember you're only going into the next room. You are only a whisper away. To me death is nothing to be afraid of. I don't want to go just now I admit because I've only just got my house and I'd like to have time to enjoy it. It would be just my luck to pop my clogs just when everything's going well!'

The atmosphere lightened and the woman smiled.

'But seriously, death is a great adventure,' I went on, 'I just hope you don't have any pain . . . Besides, how do you know how long you've got? Miracles do happen. Until the time comes I don't believe I'm going. Why don't you join our Sod It Club? Whenever

117

I'm going in for tests I say sod it, I'm not going to have it!'

Little by little the tension went out of the woman and after a few minutes she was laughing. Afterwards I got Laurie to give her my telephone number so that she could telephone me for moral support whenever she felt down, and that's how I got to know Ros quite well. It turned out we were both going into hospital for tests at the same time and afterwards I rang her to see how she'd got on. It was bad news. The cancer had spread and there didn't seem to be much hope.

'What about you, Doris,' she asked, 'have you had your results yet?'

And the words stuck in my throat. How could I tell her I was all right after she'd had such bad luck.

'Ros, I don't know how to say it. I feel dreadful after your news. But I've got the all clear.'

'Oh Doris, I'm so pleased,' she said warmly and the relief in her voice was so sincere it brought tears to my eyes. In spite of her own turmoil and tragedy she could still feel glad for me.

She was such a brave lady. That morning she said, she'd been talking to her young window cleaner whose wife had gone off and left him with a three-year-old son.

'Doris, I thought what's the matter with the world,' she said. 'There's that girl with everything to live for, a nice husband and little child and she goes away and leaves them. And here's us, such a close family and I'm being forced to leave them.'

And yet, she could still feel for that boy and sympathize with his unhappiness. That's what happens when you're getting near the spirit world. You seem to find acceptance of your own fate and a new understanding and compassion for other people.

I didn't know what I could do to help Ros so in the end I sent her a poem which had been sent to me, in the hope it would give her strength:

He Walks The Wards

If Christ came to this world again
Would He sit with those in pain?
Would he walk the hospitals at night
With tender steps so soft and light
Would he pause by each bed and pray
Hoping that He might hear you say:
'My pain is easier to bear, Christ
Now that I know you're here.'

Well, Christ is there my friend with you
He walks the ward the whole night through
He pauses by each bed to pray
So if you can, I beg you say
Your pain is easier to bear
Because you know that He is there.

Do you think that He who suffered so
Would stand aside and let you go
Through all those hours that you have passed
Pain-racked and faint yet holding fast
To life with all your bravery?
Why Christ is always there

He knows the fight you've had to wage
He alone your heart can gauge
He knows those moments when you feel
That nothing but your pain is real
He knows and lends His hands to you
To hold on till you get through

So don't give in, you mean so much
Don't ever feel you're out of touch
With life and all the folk outside
For none of them are satisfied
Unless they too can with you say
Christ passed along my life today

And in your ward and by your bed
Those words are very truly said
For Christ will ever linger near
All those who live close to a tear
And He will dry your eyes and give His Strength
   to you
So you may live within His Heart
And living there will make your pain much less to
   bear.

It makes me cry to read that poem. I think it's so beautiful. In fact I'm sent a lot of lovely poems. The most inarticulate people are suddenly touched by the spirit world and words pour out of them. Here are some of my favourites:

Mother

You always used to watch us
Anxious if we were late
In Winter by the window
In Summer by the gate.
And though we mocked you tenderly
Who took such loving care
The long road home would seem more safe
Because she waited there.
Her thoughts were all for us
She never could forget
And so I think that where she is
She must be waiting yet
Waiting till we come to her
Anxious if we're late
Watching from Heaven's window,
Leaning on Heaven's gate.

L. Lawler.

Age

Age is a quality of mind
If you have left your dreams behind
If hope is cold
If you no longer plan ahead
If your ambitions all are dead
Then you are old.

But if you make of life the best
And in your life you still have zest
If love you hold
No matter how the years go by
No matter how the birthdays fly
You are not old.

It doesn't seem so long ago
We came to say goodbye,
We held your hand and kissed your face
And had our private cry.

You looked so peaceful lying there
It was hard to realize
That when you left us here on earth
You simply closed your eyes.

So if it's true what people say
We have no cause to fear
For God will take you by the hand
And ever keep you near.

We wouldn't wish for you to stay
And suffer day by day
So when God took your hand in his
It was as if to say
No need to suffer any more
So let's quietly slip away.

Mrs Blanche Lloyd

Send Them To Bed With A Kiss

To Mothers so often discouraged,
Worn out by the toils of the day,
You often grow weary and cross and impatient,
Complain of the noise and the play,
For the play brings so many vexations,
But Mothers, whatever may vex you,
Send the children to bed with a kiss.

The dear little feet wander often,
Perhaps from the pathway of right,
The dear little hands find new mischief,
To try you from morning till night,
But think of the desolate mothers,
Who would give all the world for your bliss,
And as thanks for your infinite blessing,
Send the children to bed with a kiss.

For some day the noise will not vex you,
The silence will hurt you far more,
You will long for the sweet childish voices
For a sweet child's face at your door
And to press a child's face to your bosom,
You'd give all the world for just this,
For the comfort 'twill bring you in sorrow,
Send the children to bed with a kiss.

Shado's Poem

So small was he, so fat and round
His tummy nearly touched the ground
He stood on my hand with room to spare
Regarded me with brown eyes so aware,
Sized me up, then adopted me this special pup.

He grew in size, in wisdom too
Always seeking things to do,
The children were his special babes

None dare touch them, they were his
Love and licks and always a kiss.

Football was his special love,
Be it on the beach, on grass or on TV
He knew it all, but oh the referee
Never knew the furore he caused
When the ball was held more than a pause!

He knew his Dad was ill and tired
So kept a vigil at his side,
Those wise brown eyes so more than we
Who waited for the inevitability.

He stayed by me throughout the time
That dragged on endlessly,
Then suddenly he needed his rest,
His time had come, my special chum,
He deserved the best.

I can still see him now on that lovely plain
He'll yawn and stretch, find no more pain
That well loved voice will say to him
'Well done my son – where's Daddy's boy?'

Enjoy your new life my lovely lad,
Go walks, play games with beloved Dad,
You gave so much love to everyone,
For you the best is yet to come.

When my time to roam is over
My heart will be so happy to discover
The two of you there to wait—
One wagging his tail, one leaning on the gate!

My lovely poems may not be worthy of Shakespeare
but they bring tears to my eyes just the same. You can
tell that every one is written from the heart and springs
from the suffering and courage of personal experience.

Shado's Poem was accompanied by a moving letter from Cathie Cluff:

Dear Doris,

Thank you for all the comfort your books have brought to me ever since my beloved husband David passed over last year.

I was one of the many who were lucky enough to have a contact through you at the Usher Hall in November 1984. David was the cheeky one, in RAF Bomber Command. You were puzzled at the connection with Guy Gibson until I explained that David had flown on that Squadron. As you said 'I was Guy Gibson's driver so I know you have no connection with him – yet there is a connection!' How right you were. Right away you said 'Lancasters'.

Well, Doris, I know you occasionally like poems so hope you like this one. You see Shado adored David, never left his side towards the end and was distraught when David passed over. I had to get the vet in to him. The vet to the dog and the doctor to me – you can imagine what it was like!

I was convinced that Shado was left with me this past year to help me, too, in fact he kept my sanity. The years of nursing were taking their toll. In January of this year Shado was telling me his time had come. Arthritis had taken his rear quarters badly. So I was there too when Shado passed over. A strange thing this, Doris, don't ask me how but I know David and Shado are together again. They are company for each other and to that end, two days after Shado died, I found myself writing Shado's Poem. Thought you might like to see it.

Hope John is keeping well. I understand what hell he went through at Arnhem.

Love

Cathie Cluff.
Edinburgh.

People who sneer that a pet is 'only an animal' obviously have no idea how much comfort and love they bring, and how much sorrow the owners feel when they pass. I think a lot of readers must have been surprised to discover from my past books that animals too live on, because I get a lot of letters on this subject.

Chatham,
Kent

Dear Mrs Stokes,

I was given one of your books recently – A Host of Voices – following the death of my dog three weeks ago. Although he was only an animal, to me he was more a member of my family – a child almost, and it was a great loss when I had to have him put to sleep through throat cancer.

Reading your book gave me great comfort, not only for this loss but also for the loss of a very dear friend who committed suicide last year – and for other deaths which I must surely come up against in the future. I feel confident now that one day I will see them both again and that in the meantime my dog has got all the fields to run in he could ever want. I still say goodnight each evening because after reading your book I know he is still around.

Once again, many thanks for your help and comfort in your books. I realize that my grief must be small compared with most people's losses, but I'm glad to have found the opportunity to discover Spiritualism.

Good luck in your work and may God bless you.

Mrs B. Edwards.

Matlock
Derbyshire

Dear Mrs Stokes,

A little note to say a very big thank you. I went to the City Hall, Sheffield, on 27th November last year with many friends, and you have changed my whole life.

On 4th March our darling Rupert (cross fox terrier/poodle) passed over. I just thank God that although he was nearly 15 years of age he had had a wonderful life with quality. He was so very much loved and I long to put my arms round him and cuddle him. He loved his cuddle. I know he is only a whisper away.

Yours sincerely

Mrs V. Kembery

She is absolutely right of course. Our pets do live on and it was proved to me yet again only a couple of weeks ago.

I've already mentioned Patrick who baked the beautiful birthday cake for me and then cooked my Christmas dinner – well Patrick and I have become great friends. He pops in regularly and when he does, he always brings a little gift – a plant for the garden or some flowers for my spirit children or sometimes another cake.

'Patrick you mustn't feel you have to bring something every time you come love,' I said after a whole string of gifts had arrived. 'It's just nice to see you.'

But he insisted it gives him pleasure. He lost his mother not long ago and he likes to think of me as a substitute mum. Anyway, one particular Saturday while he was visiting me his mother came through with news that was going to be difficult to break. Apparently Patrick's beloved dog Sally was about to pass over. Oh dear, I thought. How am I going to tell him that. He loves that dog like a child.

'Patrick, love,' I said gently, 'you've got to be very brave. Your Mum's just come through and she's told me she's waiting to welcome Sally into the spirit world.'

The colour drained from Patrick's face. 'Oh no, surely not. She doesn't seem too bad.'

Sally was after all sixteen-and-a-half years old and her health was variable.

'I'm sorry Pat but that's what your mum says and if they're preparing a place for Sally it must be right. I think she'll pass over either tomorrow or Monday.'

Poor Patrick didn't know what to say. He'd known for a long time that Sally was a great age for a pekinese and couldn't last much longer, but he'd tried to pretend it wouldn't happen.

Well that night, he told me later, Sally didn't seem too bad, but the following morning she was obviously ill and by the afternoon Patrick realized she was going. Distraught he phoned me.

I tuned in straight away and his mother was there, all ready to collect the dog.

'It's her time to come to us,' she explained.

'Now Patrick be brave. You've got to let her go,' I said. 'Your Mum's come for her and it's only your love that's holding Sally back.'

Naturally Patrick was upset but he realized the poor dog was ill and it wasn't fair to try to keep her any longer.

'Pick her up in your arms,' I said, 'and say, "here you are Mum. Take her with love."'

There were some muffled sounds as Patrick put down the phone and reluctantly did as I suggested. Nothing happened at first but then he whispered, 'Go on Sally. Go to Mum.' And as he said the words Sally went limp in his arms and I had a sudden mental picture of a little honey brown dog bounding away across a sunlit meadow towards a woman who was standing with open arms.

'It's all right, Patrick,' I said when he returned speechlessly to the phone. 'She's safely over. I've seen her. She's racing around, happy and as lively as a puppy.'

The saddest letters, of course, are from parents who've lost children and it gives me special pleasure to know that I've been able to give them a little comfort in their grief.

                                        East Lothian
                                        Scotland

Dear Doris,

I hope you don't mind if I just call you Doris but you don't feel like a stranger to me, more like a trusted friend.

Our beautiful wee boy Craig passed over. I and my husband knew our wee boy was very ill, only we kept hoping and praying that it was all a bad dream and we could wake up and take him home to us, away from the hospital and just love him and look after him. Craig was only nine days old but we treasure all the beautiful memories of him and the happiness he brought to everybody.

I've always believed that when we die there is something more, that someone is looking after us. I was given your book and it seemed to lift me and reassure me in a way I can't explain very well.

The poems are beautiful and I try to remember them when the awful black despair closes in.

We love our wee boy so much. I pray we can meet him again, cuddle him and never have to part again.

You have given me the strength to really believe this.

                                        Mrs T. Johnston.

Cullompton
Devon

Dear Doris,

I expect you receive many letter like this, but I would like to say thank you so very much for making life easier for my Mum and I after having lost our little Jessica of three months in a cot death. Even though she was so young we found there was a great hole in our hearts. Twelve months have now passed but it seems like yesterday.

Until I read your books death frightened me even though I am a committed Christian. Many friends have told me it is wrong for Mum and I to believe in what you do and stand for – yet you were the one who brought comfort to our grief stricken family, knowing Jessica was being well looked after.

May God bless you both, thank you once again for being such a comfort and friend.

C Ruttey

Yarmouth
Isle of Wight

Dear Doris,

Today I listened to your Desert Island Discs programme which has very much moved me.

Forty-three years ago today, my husband of 24 years was shot down and died over Germany, flying with Bomber Command.

The child I was carrying was born in July '42 and brought all who knew and cared for her much joy, and to me much comfort. She was taken into spirit two days before her 11th birthday, 1953 after falling into an empty lift-shaft. Although I had by then other children and a fine husband I prayed to die, we had been *so* close, and I loved her *so* much.

Since then, but not at the time, I've learned much

and truly believe her short life was completed and she is with her dear father.

But for years, before my eyes I saw that white coffin going into another deep black hole.

I have passed your books to my sister who is Catholic and whose life has been transformed. Also to friends in hospital.

I can hardly see to write, having two cataracts, not to mention tears! God bless you, my dear, and give you the strength you need for your glorious mission.

Mrs B. Pense

The bulk of my letters though, are about grief in all its different forms, because of course there is not one of us who escapes grief.

Tintagel,
Cornwall

Dear Mrs Stokes,

I feel I have to write to you after seeing and hearing you on the Wogan Show last evening. Having read your books, your thoughts and experiences have given me the extra courage to face the world since my beloved husband slipped quietly away from me two years ago.

When you said you and your friend belonged to the Sod It Club how could you know that for the past 20 years or so it was my beloved's favourite expression. Oh how through the years it has relieved the tension over so many traumatic times.

Even our vicar uses it now! As indeed do all my friends.

Yours sincerely

E. Keness

Dear Doris,

Until I saw you on TV last year I'd never heard of Doris Stokes. I was overwhelmed with what I saw and very soon after I bought one of your books, read it and quickly bought and read the other three. I can't put into words the impact they had on me. You took away any fear I had of death, you explained so beautifully the continuation of life when we pass over and the more I read the more you became a personal friend.

Shortly after this wonderful happening, my mother passed over and immediately I knew she was with her loved ones who she'd earlier lost. When I left the cemetery I knew I wasn't leaving mum behind, and in the visits to her grave since, they have only been out of respect, for I know she's not there. Mum's with me whenever I want her to be, she's in my home, she's any beautiful flower, she's the brightest shining star in the sky.

You've given so much love and happiness to so many people that it makes me so happy just to write and tell you so.

Paul Russo

Bolton,
Lancs

Dear Doris (please forgive familiarity!),

I feel I must write to you after hearing your selection on Desert Island Discs yesterday morning. It was my birthday and my dear husband passed on two years ago last February and I miss him so much, especially on such anniversaries.

I was very weepy but I cannot tell you how your record selection touched me so much, for each record you picked Doris (with the exception of your own lovely verse) had a very special place for Tom and me.

I wrote them all down when you started with Lena Martell's One Day At A Time – a *special* favourite of Tom's – and then I could hardly believe my ears at all the rest of your choice. It was wonderful. Just as if dear Tom was sending me a birthday message through you.

Thank you so much. I've been so unhappy since he went but my heart was lifted for a best ever birthday present.

Yours sincerely

Mrs J. Norris

I also receive letters from children and I find it very touching to think they've struggled through my books and understood them. This is the letter from the little girl I was hoping to meet in Liverpool:

Withington
Manchester

Dear Mrs Doris Stokes,

I am writing to you because my Daddy has just died I am age 10 one time I watched television and my mummy said that you were very good and Mummy said that she would take me to see you at your house if you would let me becouse I love my Daddy ever so much and I would like to know if he is happy or sad becouse I keep on crying all the time for my Daddys love

All my love

Gale

Finally there are my 'tonic' letters. Like everybody else I get tired and fed up from time to time and when it's bitterly cold and I've got to struggle into my dress and travel miles to some theatre instead of sinking into

132

my armchair by the fire for the night, I think to myself what are you doing Doris? You must be mad.

Well I'm lucky. Because when I feel like that I've only got to read a few of my tonic letters and I know that the effort is all worthwhile.

Perranporth
Cornwall

Dear Mrs Stokes,

I felt I just had to write and thank you for such a wonderful evening last Saturday at St Austell. Having read all your books and any magazine article I could find, it became an ambition of mine to see you 'live' at one of your meetings. I found the reassurance and comfort you gave to those fortunate enough to have a sitting with you so marvellous and I'm sure most people like myself sat there spellbound!

My husband came with me on Saturday and beforehand was quite sceptical and so sure he would be able to 'see through' you. However he came away a total believer!

So thank you once again for a wonderful evening and for all the marvellous work you do.

With best wishes

Jayne Moon

A Midlands vicarage

Dear Mrs Stokes,

I am an Anglican priest and had almost lost my faith when I read your books earlier this year. You have helped me greatly and given me much more confidence in the realities of the spiritual world.

With all good wishes
(I will not embarrass him by
publishing his name)

Kingsbridge
Devon

Dear Mrs Stokes,

I have just been listening to Desert Island Discs and I feel so strongly to say what a comforting feeling it gave to me. I do so staunchly believe in a better life to come but, Doris, you made it all so clear, bless you.

My eyes aren't so good now but I read two of your books a few years ago and now, to hear you in the flesh is something I will never forget.

Yours most sincerely

Mary Winterburn

Dormansland
Surrey

Dear Doris,

I came to your evening at Croydon and I can't stop thinking or talking about it. You gave so many messages which brought so much relief, comfort and happiness not only to those to whom you were talking, but to many others present as well. The evening was a very happy one despite all the tragedies we heard about.

I have never been to a more packed theatre and the audience on leaving were very animated – hundreds of people were converging on to the car park – all talking at once.

Something happened to me during the day prior to coming to see your show. I was convinced that it was my mother's doing. Almost towards the end of your show you were talking to another spirit called Bert – you said, 'Just a minute Bert, I have a Violet coming in.' Nobody claimed Violet. Violet is my mother's name. You carried on speaking to Bert for a minute or two. Then you said, 'I have a Violet looking for Pat.'

I am Pat. I was so overcome that I just couldn't

move to speak or come down. You carried on talking to Bert again. Then you said. 'I have someone here who died of cancer of the lung.' So did my mother. Someone did claim that their father died of cancer of the lung and this message may have been for them but it did seem a coincidence.

I said to a friend that if something else happened the following day – which did seem very unlikely to both of us – then I would be convinced that the Violet you heard was my mother. This did happen so I am convinced.

Thank you Doris for all the comfort you have given in your books and also for giving us the experience of sharing in your incredible gift. It was a truly marvellous evening last Monday and one I shall never forget.

Yours sincerely

Pat Hearn

Chapter Ten

Half way through the sitting Terry put his head round the door.

'Sorry to interrupt but I'm looking for that letter from Lincoln. It's very important. Have you seen it?'

I looked at the shelving unit beside me, every surface overflowing with mail. 'Yes – well it's here somewhere.'

And I was just rummaging through when a voice from the spirit world said: 'No. It's back here,' and my hand was pushed back to the shelf behind my chair.

'Oh. No it's not,' I corrected myself. 'They've just told me it's on this shelf back here.'

I reached back and sure enough, the first letter I put my hand on was the important one from Lincoln.

'By God that's useful,' said Pat Coombs, my sitter, 'I wish I could do that. I've lost a photo album and I'm very sad about it. I wish my mother could tell me where it is.'

Her mother had been talking to us before Terry came so I tuned into the same vibration and asked. Back came a message about a garage and a chest that used to be kept there.

Pat shook her head. 'No, I've looked in the garage and it's not there.'

But her mother was insistent.

'She's really certain, Pat,' I said. 'It's in a chest that belonged to your grandparents and it was always kept in the garage. You're not to worry about it because you're going to find it very soon.'

I could see Pat was a bit sceptical about this but the sitting went on and more and more evidence came through. Her mother brought back Pat's old cat, Pip, and then she kept going on about Tiddy. I thought this must be another pet, but no, it turned out that Pat's mother's nickname was Tiddy May. She mentioned other members of the family and then suddenly a man's voice cut in. A very domineering voice.

'I was in the army,' he said.

'Oh, what rank?' I asked.

'Well you would have had to call me sir,' he chuckled. 'I was a major.'

'Yes, Tom's with me.' Tiddy May confirmed in case Pat was in any doubt that her father had arrived.

'I was always very strict and military,' he said, 'but I went peculiar towards the end. I'm glad I came over before I got incontinent. I didn't approve of Pat going into acting at first,' he added, 'but afterwards I was so proud of her. I used to say Coombs is my name. Pat Coombs' father.'

By now a great many of Pat's family and friends had come to say hello. Some of the names, however, she couldn't place. I kept getting the name Lillian which meant absolutely nothing to Pat. Back it came again and again and I was getting myself into a bit of a mess, when Ramanov took pity on me.

'It's not Lillian,' he said, 'it's Lally.'

Pat recognized it at once. 'Lally Bowers! An old actress friend of mine.'

There was also an answer to a tragic mystery. A young man called Nicholas joined us, bringing with him a feeling of confusion.

'My nephew,' said Pat.

He mentioned Kings Cross in Sydney, Australia, where he'd lived and also talked of Brighton. Brighton, Australia? I queried. 'No. Brighton-on-Sea, England,' he said.

'That's quite right,' said Pat, 'we used to live there and he came to visit us.'

Nicholas should not have passed over when he did he kept telling me. It shouldn't have happened. There was a great deal of confusion surrounding his last hours on earth. There was something about a car.

'I was thrown,' he said, 'that's the last thing I remember. I was thrown.'

'Nobody knows what happened,' said Pat. 'His body was found beside a road in Australia. He had head injuries but apart from that there wasn't a mark on him.'

From what Nicholas said it sounded as if it wasn't an accident. The poor boy was an epileptic and it may have been that he started to have a fit and the occupants of the car, thinking he was turning violent, opened the door and pushed him out.

By the end of the sitting Pat was even more fascinated than she'd been when she arrived and she stayed on chatting for most of the afternoon. She was particularly pleased by something that sounded almost like a prediction from the other side, although I always stress that I don't tell fortunes.

I heard the name Agatha Christie very strongly and at the same time I got a very clear impression of Pat moving away from comedy.

'Pat, people associate you with comedy,' I said, 'but from what they're telling me, you could do much meatier roles. I'm getting the name Agatha Christie.'

'Oh God, I'd love to do Agatha Christie,' Pat agreed.

'Who's Michael?' I asked suddenly.

'He's a writer friend. He adapts things.'

'Well I think Michael might have something to do with you appearing in Agatha Christie. You'd make a wonderful Miss Marple,' and as I said it a vivid picture of Pat as Miss Marple with a battered hat, a bicycle and a cat round her ankles flashed into my mind.

'Let's hope you're right, Doris,' said Pat, 'I'd love to play Miss Marple. I really would.'

Most extraordinary of all the things she'd heard from the spirit world as far as Pat was concerned though was the affair of the photo album.

When she got home that afternoon she phoned her sister to tell her what happened.

'But when I got to the part about the photo album she went very quiet,' Pat told me afterwards. 'It turned out she'd found the album that very morning in a sort of treasure chest that belonged to our grandmother. The chest was under her bed but before it passed to her it probably had been stored in the garage for years.'

People are often astonished by the accuracy of the spirit world, even more so where figures are involved. I'm not quite sure why. After all, all the messages that I hear quite distinctly are correct, so why some truths should seem more impressive than others I don't know. I remember once at a public demonstration the spirit world remarked that a woman in the audience had just bought a new oven and she'd got £130 off the recommended price. The audience were amazed when this turned out to be absolutely correct. Yet when another woman was told that a relative had just had a baby and was given the correct name, the audience seemed almost to take it for granted. I couldn't help feeling puzzled. Surely both pieces of evidence were equally good?

Something similar happened recently. A couple who'd lost their much loved daughter, Sarah, came for a sitting. The wife seemed very keen but the husband was highly sceptical and I got the impression he was only there on sufferance to please his wife. Throughout the conversation with Sarah, he sat there looking perplexed, as if he knew there was a catch somewhere but he couldn't work out where. Then towards the end, Sarah said that she'd left £28 behind to buy her brother, Chris, a present.

'Well we can soon settle that,' said her mother, 'I've got her pay packet here. I've not opened it yet.'

And she opened her handbag, brought out a battered envelope, tore off the top and shook out the contents. Onto her knee fell several notes and some loose change. She counted it. There was exactly £28.20.

At this the father shook his head in wonder.

'There was just no way you could have known,' he said. 'Even we didn't know . . .'

Even Laurie, who sees these things happen all the time, is sometimes shaken. Not long ago we were talking about Marc Bolan. I'd once contacted Marc on the other side during a sitting and it turned out that Laurie knew Marc on this side and that his brother used to work with him.

'He was such a nice guy,' said Laurie, 'd'you know he even left Alphi £5,000 in his will. Unfortunately when it came to it there wasn't enough money in the estate to pay out so Alphi didn't get anything, but it didn't matter. He was really touched to know that Marc remembered him.'

I was just about to agree what a nice thoughtful boy Marc was, when suddenly Marc himself arrived.

'He's had the money now, Doris,' Marc assured me, 'and he got £6,000 not £5,000.'

'Laurie, Marc's just told me Alphi's had the money,' I said quickly, 'and it was £6,000.'

Laurie shook his head. 'No, love. You're wrong somewhere. This was years ago and there wasn't enough money to pay Alphi. He didn't get a thing.'

Well I didn't pursue it. It wasn't important and Alphi's affairs were none of my business. I didn't even give it another thought until a couple of days later, Laurie phoned me in great excitement.

'You'll never guess, Doris, I've just had a call from Alphi. He wants to take my wife and I out to celebrate. The money from Marc Bolan's come through and he did get £6,000. Marc left him £5,000 but the interest has been building up all these years and it's £6,000 now.'

Laurie himself has never had a sitting with me. Night after night at theatre demonstrations he meets so many people desperate for a sitting that he feels it would be wrong to ask me to use up my psychic energy to satisfy curiosity when there are more urgent cases out there than I could ever hope to get through in a lifetime. Nevertheless I sometimes come out with little bits without realizing it.

One morning when he called in, I asked him if he'd mind taking a bundle of clothes we no longer wear down to the Oxfam Shop or the Salvation Army for the old folk. Laurie didn't mind at all and we were just stuffing them into large carrier bags, when a woman's voice suddenly said: 'Tell him to take them round to Issy's.'

'You're to take them round to Issy's, Laurie,' I repeated out loud.

Laurie stopped dead, a pair of trousers poised in mid-air.

'What did you say?'

'It's your Mum, love,' I explained, 'she's just come over and said you're to take the clothes round to Issy's. What's Issy's?'

Laurie looked flabbergasted. 'I can't believe it. When we were kids in the East End my Mum used to take us to Issy Goodyear's in the Roman Road to buy second-hand clothes. I've not even thought about Issy's for years. The place must have been knocked down thirty years ago!'

He was so thrilled to hear from his mother that he phoned his wife, Iris, straight away to tell her the news.

'I couldn't have better proof that my old Mum was there,' he said. 'No one else would ever have known of Issy's.'

Yes, it's certainly true that occasionally the spirit world can help you find things or give you information that you want, which as Pat Coombes said, is very useful, and it's for this reason I'm sometimes asked to work on police cases. When I was in New Zealand last, I was asked to help find a missing girl. She gave her name, Susan, and she described the landscape she remembered in her last moments, but it was wintertime and the whole area was covered by snow. Later when the snows had cleared the police went back and searched the place and sure enough they found the body. I had pinpointed within 500 yards, the motorway where she was picked up and last seen alive.

But I must stress that it doesn't always work. Sometimes the messages are too confused, sometimes the significance of the information doesn't dawn until after the case is solved – like the time I was given the name Sutcliffe during a sitting with the parents of Jayne MacDonald, one of the victims of the Yorkshire Ripper. Mrs McDonald said it was an old family name and we thought no more about it until the Ripper was caught and he turned out to be a man called Peter Sutcliffe – and sometimes the spirit world deliberately withholds information if it would do more harm than good.

I remember recently the police brought a man to see me whose seventeen-year-old daughter had been raped and murdered. Naturally they were after any clues they could get to the identity of the killer but I just couldn't help. The distraught father sat there on the sofa willing me to come up with a name and all I could feel was hate and the desire for revenge. The poor child came back and tried to talk to her father.

'I was a good girl, you know,' she kept saying. 'Tell him I was a good girl.'

But I didn't feel he was properly listening. He didn't so much want contact with his daughter as a name to pin on his hatred.

The violence of the atmosphere washed over me in wave after wave until I eventually faltered.

'Ask her who did it. Ask his name,' insisted the father, knuckles white, teeth clenched. 'Who did it, who did it?'

But from the spirit world there was only silence.

'It's no good,' I said at last, 'they're not going to

give me his name because if I tell you I know what you'd do. You'd get up from that sofa, get in the car, find that boy and kill him.'

'Yes, that's right. I would,' said the father.

Many fathers in similar situations must have threatened the same thing but this man really meant it. These were no empty words.

'Well,' I said, 'the spirit world won't help you do it. What good would it do? What would happen to your wife and children with you in prison? Because that's what would happen to you.'

He wouldn't listen. 'I'll worry about that,' he said. 'Just give me his name.'

But his relatives on the other side had more sense. They refused to be a party to his plans and although they probably knew the answer, they said not a word.

'I'm sorry,' I apologized to the policeman at the end of the sitting, 'I can't help you. It might work with another member of the family but I'm afraid the father's blocking it.'

In desperate circumstances of course I try to help because there's always the chance that the tiniest scrap of information might lead to the capture of a killer and prevent another murder, but I stress strongly that I can't guarantee anything.

Not long ago I received a telephone call from the *Sevenoaks Chronicle* asking if I could help find a missing person. I explained the problems but they were still keen to try. I didn't know the details and I didn't want to but I gathered the case was something of a mystery and the normal channels had failed. I was a last resort. We could well be dealing with a murder, I realized, so I agreed to do what I could.

The reporter came along with a tiny, nervous looking middle-aged lady who was clearly at her wits' end with trying to solve the puzzle. They set up a tape recorder, the reporter got out her notebook and once we were all settled in armchairs with a cup of coffee close by, I tuned in.

143

At once my head was full of German voices. I don't understand German but I knew instinctively that German was the language I was hearing.

'I hear German being spoken,' I began uncertainly.

'That's right,' said my sitter, 'I'm German.'

And in fact she did have a faint trace of an accent but her English was so good it was impossible to say where she originated from.

Oh well, I thought, I suppose I'll have to ask Ramanov to translate the whole thing for me, but to my surprise the atmosphere changed and the rest of the evidence came spontaneously in English.

Now I could understand what was said but it didn't seem to make any sense.

'Yugoslavia,' said a distant voice and I got a confused image of mountains. Now why, when we'd just established the German connection, was I getting information about Yugoslavia, I wondered.

'I'm hearing something about Yugoslavia, mountains and things,' I said, 'so there must be a connection there.'

'Yes, that's right,' said the woman.

Then I was surrounded by darkness and I didn't know what was going on. Out of the black the man's voice came again.

'Anna,' he said.

'That's me,' said the woman eagerly.

'And who's Willie?'

'That's my husband.'

Instinctively I understood that it was her husband who was missing and I was pretty sure it was Willie I was talking to on the other side, although he hadn't said so in so many words. I was very reluctant to come right out and say that he'd definitely passed over, however – I always am in cases like these. I will never forget the war years when John was missing, presumed dead and a medium had told me that he was definitely on the other side, when in fact he was

144

wounded and lying in hospital in a prisoner-of-war camp.

We can all make mistakes and sometimes the voices are muddled and indistinct. There are times when you might think you've made contact with a particular person when in fact you're tuned in to a member of their family who's talking about them.

I find it best to keep an open mind, repeat what I'm hearing and leave it to the sitter to decide if it sounds like the person they've lost.

'Anneliesse,' said the voice in my ear.

'Who's Anneliesse?' I asked.

'That's my full name,' said the woman, 'but everyone calls me Anna.'

It was sounding more and more as if it was indeed her husband I was talking to.

'I feel there's a great mystery and a lot of confusion,' I went on. 'I feel as if I'm falling. I feel as if he was walking in the mountains and you weren't with him.'

Willie was getting agitated. 'I left everything behind in the hotel,' he said. 'Some people say it must have been planned, but how could it? I left everything behind. My clothes, everything.'

Once more there was an impression of darkness and then a drop. I struggled to keep hold of the vibration. It was really frustrating. The impressions were so confused I could hardly make head or tail of what was coming through. From somewhere a long way off came a hard 'k' sound. A name.

'Carl . . . Kurt . . .' I tried.

'Kurt,' said the woman, 'he lives in Sevenoaks. He's worked very hard to try to find Willie.'

But I hardly heard her voice. Suddenly I was on a rocky path and very loud I could hear the sound of rushing water. Not far away there was a waterfall.

Now at last we were getting somewhere. This, I felt sure, was significant.

'I can hear water rushing,' I explained out loud, 'and there's a drop close by and a waterfall. And this man who's talking to me, he has a very loving voice. He isn't the type to just disappear. He says he had only been there three days and if he'd wanted to disappear he would have gone on the first day. He just went out and never returned.'

'Katarina,' said the man emphatically.

'Who's Katarina?' I asked.

'She's a Yugoslav girl who was there,' said the woman.

She too was important. The man was obviously anxious to prove that he hadn't planned to run away, neither had he been suicidal.

'Ask Katarina,' he said, 'she will tell you I was perfectly all right. I wasn't depressed.'

And then there was the rushing water again. The sound was in the background the whole time. If I closed my eyes it would have been difficult to believe I was sitting in my own armchair in my own sitting-room. I felt as if I was high on a mountainside beside a stream. And there was the waterfall again. There was something about that waterfall . . .

'He's saying you go up the path before the fall, then there's a drop,' I said slowly. 'And it's a big fall . . .'

But my contact couldn't seem to hold the impression steady. I was getting the sounds all right but the pictures kept going. The rocky path disappeared and instead I got a name.

'Wolfgang.'

The woman gave a little gasp. 'That's Willie's real name – but nobody knew. Everybody called him Willie.'

The man was getting agitated again. He had a very orderly mind and he seemed to feel that the search hadn't been thorough enough.

'He gets very impatient,' I explained. 'He can't understand why they are so lax. He says they only have to go five paces and they would find him. He seems to think they've stopped bothering in Yugo-slavia.'

Another impression flickered before my eyes. I was bending down to look at something interesting, some plant I think and then something hit me on the back of the head. The sound of running water continued but in addition I got a fleeting glimpse of caves.

'He was climbing just before the waterfall and stopped to look at something that interested him,' I said out loud. 'Further up the mountain there are caves . . . I don't think the caves have been searched properly.'

The sitting went on. There were more names. The man mentioned Derek, his son, and Jenny the cat and he even asked about his white car. I was pretty certain from the way he was talking that he was the missing husband and he'd been killed in suspicious circumstances. I couldn't think why but there seemed to be some sort of cover-up somewhere.

'Well, what do you think, love?' I asked Anneliesse when the power eventually faded. 'D'you think we've been talking to your husband.'

'Oh yes,' she said. 'It sounded just like him.'

Afterwards the reporter filled me in on the story. Apparently the couple were called Mr and Mrs Bleyberg and they had been going to Yugoslavia on walking holidays for the past twenty years or so. They always went to the same area and they knew the hotel and locals quite well. They could even speak some of the language.

Willie was a respected science teacher in Sevenoaks, Kent, and the couple lived a quiet, ordinary life. Then in July 1984 when the time for their holiday came round again, Anneliesse's mother was ill and she had to stay behind to look after her. Anneliesse wasn't keen on her husband going away alone but he seemed to have his heart set on this holiday so reluctantly she agreed.

The morning he disappeared was fine and bright and Willie breakfasted at the hotel and set out for his walk straight afterwards. He left his personal belongings behind in his room and gave every indication that he would be returning for dinner.

Later in the day two locals saw him on the mountain alone but cheerful, and an hour or two afterwards they bumped into him again. He'd tried one particular path he told them but it was too difficult so he was going to set out in a different direction. Off he went with a good-natured wave and was never seen again.

The extraordinary part of the story was that Anneliesse wasn't informed that her husband was missing until five days later. The area was searched but nothing was found, and to add to her distress, Anneliesse realized that without a body she couldn't prove that her husband was dead and all his financial affairs would be frozen until a death certificate was issued – which couldn't be done, of course, without a body.

The muddle and the uncertainty, added to her natural grief, was proving almost too much for the poor woman. The only consolation was that the evidence from the sitting might be enough to persuade the authorities to reopen the case and call for another search.

Yes, the spirit world does often help us find things – but it's not a one-way affair. Sometimes they want us to help them!

I was doing a couple of demonstrations in Bridlington not long ago and I had been looking forward to it. After the long cold winter and several doses of 'flu, a breath of sea air was just what I needed. We were staying in a nice seaside hotel and that first night I was hoping for a long refreshing sleep.

Well I had the refreshing sleep all right, but it wasn't very long! Early in the morning, just as the dawn chorus was starting up, I heard a voice talking to me.

'It's Paul. I hung myself,' he said.

Half asleep, I thought I was having a nightmare. I peeped out through slits in my eyelids and saw that

148

I was quite safe in my comfortable hotel room. I'm dreaming I said to myself and turned over for another hour or two.

'I hung myself,' said the sad voice again. And this time I realized it was no use. I couldn't pretend. I wasn't asleep and I wasn't dreaming. The voice was real.

I sat up. 'You what, love? What did you say?'

'I hung myself,' said the boy. 'Can you tell my Mum I'm sorry? She's so upset.'

'Well how am I going to find your Mum, love?' I asked. There was no telling where he came from or anything.

From the other side I could feel a great effort being made. The lad couldn't have been over very long and he was having difficulty keeping the power going.

'Paul,' I heard again. Then, 'Plane Street.'

There was silence for a long time and then just when I thought he'd gone there came the name 'Hewson', very faint.

'I was twenty,' he added. 'Shane's got my things.'

That was it. Well it wasn't much to go on. How on earth was I going to find Paul's Mum. I had part of an address but Plane Street on its own wasn't much use without a town to go with it.

Luckily later that day I had an interview booked with a reporter from the Hull *Daily Mail*. Perhaps she might have heard something. After all if it had happened recently it might have been in the paper.

When she arrived I explained what had happened.

'I got the name Paul, and Hewson and Plane Street,' I said. 'He said he hanged himself and that he was only twenty. Does that ring any bells? D'you think Plane Street could be in your area?'

She shook her head. 'No, it doesn't mean anything to me, Doris. I don't remember a story like that, but I'll check with the paper if you like.'

She rang through to her office and we waited while they flicked through back copies of the paper. Then

149

ten minutes later they found the item. On the previous Saturday a boy named Paul Hewson hanged himself. He lived in Plane Street. They couldn't confirm whether there was anybody in the family called Shane, but Paul was only twenty years old. Now all I needed was the Hewsons to be present at my demonstration that night and I could do as Paul had asked.

Well it didn't work out quite as neatly as that but it wasn't bad. Mrs Hewson wasn't in the audience that night but her cousin was. I gave her some flowers to take home to Paul's Mum and I explained that if Mrs Hewson would like to come to the demonstration the following night, we'd arrange it. Thank goodness we were doing two nights in Bridlington!

Sure enough, Mrs Hewson wanted to come and during the second half of the demonstration Paul came back, clear and strong. His practise the morning before had obviously helped him get the hang of communicating.

Mrs Hewson came to the microphone as the message began and gradually she was joined by more and more people.

'He's still talking about Shane,' I said as we began.

'Yes, Shane's his brother,' said Mrs Hewson.

'And he tells me he's being buried at three o'clock on Friday.'

'That's right.'

'Who's Donna?'

'His girlfriend.'

Dabbing quickly at her eyes, a very young girl came to the microphone. 'Donna and I were going to get engaged you know,' Paul said proudly.

'Yes, we were,' she sobbed.

Then Paul spotted someone else he knew. 'There's Dave. There's my mate!' he cried in delight. 'He's in my group.'

It turned out Paul was a drummer in a pop group and his friend Dave had been very close to him.

Dave stepped forward to join Mrs Hewson and Donna.

'We were doing so well with the group and Donna and I were going to get engaged. I must have been mad. I must have been off my trolley to do it,' Paul went on.

'Apparently he had words with someone, Dave, about a gig,' I explained. 'He was a very likeable boy but very sensitive and someone upset him.'

But Paul didn't want to dwell on the unhappiness. 'My guvnor's here tonight as well,' he confided, 'Frank.'

Sure enough, Frank was there and grinning bashfully he came out of the audience to join the little crowd round the mike.

'I'll always be with Frank in the car,' said Paul. 'When he's out in the motor tell him to think of me and I'll be there.'

'Yes we were often together in the car,' said Frank, 'I used to run him around.'

Most of all though, Paul was concerned about his brother Shane. I couldn't quite work out what he meant. He seemed to want Shane to have something that belonged to him but I couldn't catch what it was and Mrs Hewson couldn't think of anything that seemed likely.

'Well I don't know quite what he means,' I admitted, 'but I know he's very concerned about Shane. He says it frightened Shane badly.'

Mrs Hewson nodded. 'Shane hasn't broken down yet, you see,' she said. This was a bad sign. When people don't cry it means the pain and bitterness turns inwards and can make them ill. No wonder Paul was worried.

'Well give him something of Paul's and tell him that Paul wants him to have it with his love,' I said. 'It might help.'

And, finally, right at the end Paul told me that they were having a beautiful set of drums made in flowers for his funeral.

'Thank them for that, I shall enjoy it,' he said, 'but tell Mum not to spend too much money.'

I couldn't devote the whole evening to Paul's people, of course, because it wasn't a private sitting and other families wanted a turn too. I had to move on. But at least Paul had been able to prove to his mother that he wasn't dead, that he was still taking an interest in the family and above all that he was sorry for the heartache he caused.

Chapter Eleven

It was spring, though you'd never have guessed it from the weather, and there we were back on our travels, gliding down the motorway in our posh limousine heading for Cornwall.

The rain was streaming down the windows, the wipers slapping like mad but our voices drowned out the storm as we sang along lustily to *Sing Something Simple*.

Maybe it was the flat countryside we were passing through or maybe it was the tune I was croaking, but suddenly my memory did a backward somersault – the years rolled away and I was bowling along in the battered old Morris E with running boards on the side that we'd bought for £32. Terry couldn't have been more than four in those days and we couldn't afford holidays, but it didn't matter.

On fine summer Sundays we used to get up at the crack of dawn, load the Morris and head off to Skegness, our nearest seaside resort – sixty miles away. We'd drive as far as our empty stomachs would allow, and then when we couldn't stand it any longer, we'd pull up in a pretty spot, get out the little spirit stove and I'd cook breakfast at the side of the road. Later, on the beach, we paddled with Terry, and John took him in swimming. Then at the end of a long happy day we'd drive back, singing along to *Sing Something Simple* at the top of our voices.

I sighed and wiped condensation from the window. Here we were forty years on swanning round in a Daimler and staying at the best hotels, yet we'd never been so happy as those days when we rattled off to the seaside in our £32 Morris and had to stop and think twice about whether we could afford to buy an ice cream for Terry.

There's something about travelling that sparks off memories and when I'm anywhere near Lincolnshire, the floodgates really open. Grantham, of course, is my home town and although it's changed a lot since I was a girl it's still like stepping into a time machine when I go back.

The last time I was there I met my long lost cousin Ron Sutton and when he walked in my stomach did a sudden flip, because these days he looks so much like my father it was as if Dad had come into the room. You can certainly tell Ron's a Sutton all right.

He's a great character is Ron. Everyone in Grantham knows him. Sixty-nine years old, he jumps fences like a two-year-old and races around on his moped in his leather jacket and crash helmet. The effect is a bit spoiled by the fact that Ron doesn't wear any teeth, but when people ask where they are he says: 'I left them in a jam jar when we lived in Norton Street. I suppose they were still there when they pulled the houses down.'

He's not at all bothered. 'I can eat whatever I like. Pickled onions, anything,' he insists and he can as well. He must have very tough gums.

In his time Ron has been known to do a bit of poaching – just like my father. When I was a little girl my father once disappeared for a week and I was told he'd gone to Lincoln. This was quite true, but I didn't find out until I was older that he'd actually been sent to Lincoln prison for poaching.

In those days we were very poor and it was quite common for people to do a bit of poaching to make ends meet. My father was quite open about it.

'Yes and I'd go to prison for 7 days again rather than see my family go hungry when Lord Brownlow's got all those rabbits running wild on his land,' he used to say.

It all came back as Ron stood grinning in the

154

reception of the George Hotel, his crash helmet dangling from his hand.

'I've just been to the sales,' he told me. 'By – there was some good stuff going for little or nothing.'

And once again it could have been my father talking. Dad loved auctions and what we called 'the stones' in the market. Grantham is an old market town and on Saturday the farmers used to bring all their produce in. There was cattle one side, then all the pets, puppies and kittens and caged birds, then the big furniture and then the small stuff laid out 'on the stones' – small areas enclosed by railings with tables full of boxes in the centre.

Dad used to gravitate towards the stones and what he was after was clocks. He had a thing about clocks. We had so many clocks in our house it was incredible. You must have heard the place ticking like a time bomb from right up the street. When I look back now I think why on earth didn't we keep them? They'd be worth a fortune now. There were chiming clocks and grandfather clocks, you name it and we'd got it. Dad used to get them cheap if they didn't go. He fiddled until he got them working and then, as often as not, if someone admired a particular clock he said, 'Well you can have it.'

He gave them all away.

But no matter how many clocks we had, Dad just couldn't resist the market. In fact he loved it so much that he carried on visiting from the other side, as I happen to know.

Like everyone else in Grantham, John and I used to do our shopping in the market on Saturday. There was an old saying in Grantham that if you wanted to meet any of your old pals you haven't seen for years, go down to Grantham market on a Saturday and sure enough, somewhere or other you'll bump into them.

Well John and I with Terry in tow used to shop and chat then we'd wander up to the auctions on the stones for a look round. One particular day we were standing

155

peering through the railings when I noticed a large cardboard box standing on the table inside. You weren't allowed to examine it, you were expected to bid and hope for the best. It seemed crazy. I mean who'd bid for a cardboard box without knowing what was inside?

I was just shaking my head at such madness when I heard my father's voice clear as clear.

'Bid for that box, Dol,' he said firmly.

And I didn't hesitate. When my Dad used that tone of voice you did as you were told – even if it was over thirty years since he'd passed.

'I'm going to bid for that box, John,' I announced loudly.

John stared at me as if I'd been out in the sun too long. 'Don't be a fool. You don't know what's in it.'

'I know, but I'm going to bid for it,' I insisted, and I went right ahead.

There were obviously quite a few people as reckless as me because the bidding went up and up and eventually it reached ten shillings, which was a lot of money in those days. Ten shillings! I thought with the first pang of anxiety. But Dad had told me to do it and he must have seen something in that box that was a bargain.

I shot my hand up. 'Yes ten shillings!' I called in case they hadn't noticed my hand.

And miraculously everyone else dropped out and the box was mine. John shook his head in disbelief, quite speechless at such extravagance, and I must admit I had a few qualms myself.

'Suppose it's full of old clothes or plaster ornaments,' I thought in horror. But I held my head high and handed over my ten shillings as confidently as if I knew for a fact that the box was full of treasure. All the way home I had a nasty fluttery feeling in my stomach and I raced inside as soon as John opened the door.

Down went the box on the kitchen table and rapidly I tore open the top and ripped out the newspaper

156

packing. Then I relaxed and a great big grin spread over my face. Good old Dad. He hadn't let me down.

'John, look at this!' I called and I pulled out of the box a silver Queen Anne tea service, followed by a set of silver cutlery with beautiful carved ivory handles.

That box was a godsend. It went under my bed and whenever we were really hard up I rummaged through for a piece of silver to sell. My silver got us through quite a few difficult times.

I'm sure Dad continued to go to the sales with us because a year or so later the same thing happened again, only this time it wasn't a cardboard box but a sealed jewellery box he told me to bid for. When I got it home I discovered it was filled with pretty pieces of jewellery.

I don't suppose they were worth a fortune but they brought in a shilling or two when I was at my wits' end and didn't know how we'd manage till the end of the week.

Ron and I had a wonderful time catching up on the old days. There was a time when his house had been like a second home to me and Ron's mum, Aunt Aggie, was very good to me when I was a little girl. She had a thing about lace did Aunt Aggie and she had lace draped over her pictures and mirrors and lace draped along the mantelshelf. In fact anywhere you could drape lace, Aunt Aggie draped it.

She was very kind. The first thing she said when you crossed the threshold was, 'Are you hungry? Have you eaten girl?' And there was always something to eat even if it was only a piece of bread and dripping. And when I was fourteen and just started work and came home with my hands all chapped and bleeding from scrubbing floors, it was Aunt Aggie who rubbed them with vaseline and bandaged them up for me.

So I was astonished when I came out of the hotel, climbed into the Daimler and waved goodbye to Ron one day, when a lady said to me, 'How on earth did you get a relative like Ron Sutton?'

I just stared at her in amazement. I come from a poor background and I'm not ashamed to admit it. I'm proud of being a Sutton, just like Ron. It's made me hard-working and self-reliant. Years ago when he came home from Arnhem with a head wound, John found he couldn't work in the factory. The noise of the machines was driving him mad. He needed peace and quiet and the open air, so he took a job as a gardener at a private school just outside Stamford.

Accommodation was provided and I was to do a bit of everything – cleaning, standing in for matron, a little cooking now and again. At the interview we'd been shown a pleasant little flat inside the main building, but when we arrived with our furniture, having given up the house we'd been renting, the owner announced that she couldn't allow a man in the place with the girls, so she was putting us in the coach house.

Well we couldn't believe our eyes. The place had previously been used as a stable. There were rats as big as cats and no proper cooking facilities. Another woman might have turned right round and gone straight back to Grantham and who could blame her – but I was a Sutton and Suttons, I decided, stuck it out. We'd burned our boats in Grantham. Factory work was making John ill. We'd just have to make the best of it.

I scrubbed the place from the top to bottom. I made do and I learned how to make Yorkshire puddings in a frying pan on an upturned electric fire. We survived and we stuck it out for six months until John found something better.

That was the way I was brought up and Ron too and no matter what material things we collect along the years we're still the same people. So why on earth shouldn't I have a cousin like Ron Sutton?

Yes travel does send me off down memory lane but that's not to say that the present isn't every bit as interesting as the past. Cornwall turned out to be just

158

as pretty as people told me it would be. The hedgerows were full of buttery primroses, there were daffodils in every garden and the little thatched cottages really did look like chocolate box lids come to life. It was a pity about the rain but through the flowing windows you could tell it would be beautiful when the sun came out.

There had been a bit of difficulty booking a hotel. Laurie had found a conveniently situated place but when he phoned they sounded doubtful.

'Are you a group?' asked the receptionist.

'I suppose so,' said Laurie, 'there are four of us.'

The receptionist wasn't sure this counted. 'You'll have to ask the manager,' she said.

The manager wasn't too encouraging either.

'Doris Stokes,' he said. 'Never heard of her.'

Nevertheless, he agreed that if Laurie sent in written confirmation it would be all right. Well Laurie wrote his letter but just before we left some niggling doubt made him phone the hotel again, just to make sure.

It was a good thing he did, because the rooms had been let to other people.

Perhaps it was a simple mistake, but I got the feeling that the manager didn't want the likes of us staying there. Maybe he thought I'd bring ghosts into the hotel, or hold weird seances in my room!

Undaunted Laurie found us another place in Newquay, but I was a little anxious about the reception we'd receive. Perhaps we wouldn't be welcome in Cornwall.

It just shows how wrong you can be. They couldn't have been nicer at the hotel in Newquay. The manageress herself came to greet us, apologizing profusely because her hands were grubby.

'I've just been potting up some plants in the greenhouse,' she explained. Then she peered at our tired faces, bleary from the seven hour journey. 'You look as if you could do with some tea,' she said. 'Come and get settled and I'll bring you a pot. I've put Mr and Mrs

159

Stokes in the villa because we've got a wedding tonight and it'll be quieter away from the main building,' and she led us outside, chatting as if we were old friends come to stay.

The villa turned out to be a pleasant little house in the grounds and we'd hardly put down our suitcases before the manageress was back with a tray of tea.

'Now don't forget. If there's anything you want just call.'

It was a hectic visit. We'd travelled to Cornwall to do a charity show in aid of the Save the Children Fund at a school hall in St Austell, where we were also to be presented with a cheque for the same cause. There were a frantic few moments when Laurie found that the man who'd organized the whole thing and made all the arrangements couldn't be reached at the telephone number we'd been given. We had panicky visions of having come all this way for nothing, when Ramanov stepped in with some sensible advice.

'Get in touch with the radio station. They will find him.'

'Brilliant,' said Laurie and sure enough little more than an hour after the SOS went out over the local radio, the organizer phoned us.

While we were in Cornwall there was one sitting I had to do. Apparently there was a girl who'd been trying every way she could think of to get a sitting. She'd even written to *Jim'll Fix It*. I didn't feel I could turn her away after that, particularly as I was going to be in the area, so I invited her to come and see me.

Well three of them turned up, Phyllis, who'd written the letter, and two other girls, Pat and Nicola. It was a right old mix up, with spirit people wanting to talk to all of them, but we managed to sort most of it out. It turned out that Phyllis' husband, Peter, had died suddenly of a heart attack while he was playing badminton and Peter was related to Pat.

'That's my sister,' he told me.

Peter's parents, Bertram and Ivy, came back too, to say hello and then I kept hearing a strange word. It sounded very like 'Catshole'. I tried to ignore it but they kept sending it back to me. Well I didn't know what to make of it. It sounded a bit rude to me but they were so insistent, I decided to risk it.

'Look I don't know what to make of this,' I admitted, 'but I'm hearing something like Catshole. I don't know what it means . . .'

'Yes Catshole!' exclaimed Pat in delight. 'It's a place. We used to live there!'

They seemed quite pleased with the sitting but there was no time to hang around, we had to be off to St Austell. I changed into my long dress, climbed back into the car and we set off down tiny lanes with steep green banks on either side. It was still raining. If it carries on like this I'll need flippers not a long dress, I said to myself. I'd long since given up worrying about my hair. In damp weather it goes just like a gollywog and I must have looked like something the cat dragged in. But in St Austell it didn't matter a bit. We had such a wonderful evening, there was so much love generated in that school building that if you could have connected it to the national grid we'd have lit up Cornwall!

They'd gone to a great deal of trouble with the stage and it looked magnificent. They must have emptied six flower shops. There were tubs and tubs of daffodils and great baskets of flowers for me to give away. It glowed bright gold even with the lights turned down and when the spotlights came on it was radiant.

Nobody was left out. As the audience came in they were presented with white carnations and I was given a beautiful spray of yellow roses.

The atmosphere was wonderful from the start and the voices flowed. One in particular stands out in my mind because it was a lesson for all of us.

A boy named Richard came through, very distressed because he'd taken his own life. He was looking for Lynne he said and Stephen went with Lynne.

A woman came forward at once.

'I'm Lynne,' she said, 'Stephen's my son and Richard's my son in spirit.'

'Richard's very distressed,' I began tactfully.

'Yes, Doris,' said the woman, 'he shot himself.'

She seemed quite composed so I went on.

'He's got a girl with him.'

'Yes that'll be my daughter, she drowned.'

I paused unable to quite believe all the tragedy I was hearing. 'And there's another young person just joined them who's just gone over and . . . Oh dear, don't say he took himself over as well . . .'

'Yes,' said the woman, 'that's my nephew, Kevin. He took his own life three days ago.'

The horror grew. More and more names came through and the woman recognized them all, reeling off their sad stories one by one, 'Oh yes he took himself over, she did it . . .' Until in the end I was almost speechless. What tragedy some people suffer, I thought, and yet this lady's face was serene and she managed to smile.

'Well like you, Doris, I take one day at a time,' she said, 'there must be a reason for it.'

I had to admire such courage. What a marvellous attitude. She was absolutely right of course, but in the same situation I don't know if I would have had the strength just to trust and believe that everything happened for a reason.

There was great love and unselfishness that night. Later I got the name Maria.

'Who's Maria?' I asked.

'I am,' said an Italian woman walking down to the microphone.

I got her son back and as I was talking to him I felt something cool and knobbly put into my hand. It was a rosary.

'He's put a rosary into my hand,' I said, 'so I know you must have put one in with him.'

Maria broke down. 'That's it, it's all I wanted to

know,' she sobbed in relief, quite content to move aside and let someone else have a turn now she'd got the one piece of evidence that proved to her her son was still close.

The same unselfish attitude touched everyone. They held a raffle for a beautiful doll during the evening and later when I was having a cup of tea in one of the classrooms, the winner asked if she could come and see me. She came in, tears streaming down her face, the magnificent doll in her arms.

'Doris, my little girl's only sixteen months old, too young for this,' she said, 'I'd like you to have it for the Save the Children Fund.'

The doll was exquisite, all done up in silver organzine but, I thought, a child would sooner have a doll she can undress. So when we got home I asked a clever friend to make a set of clothes and underwear that could be taken off and put on again, so that I could give the doll to the bone marrow unit at Westminster Hospital for some frightened little girl to play with.

There were more lovely surprises at St Austell. When the demonstration was over, two little children came on stage carrying a giant £2,000 cheque between them, just like the giant pools cheques you see on television. They presented it to me for the Save the Children Fund, then off they went, only to return with Tracey, the little girl staggering under the weight of a huge box of Cornish goodies and Stephen the little boy, carrying a breakfast set of Cornish pottery. Gifts from Cornwall for me to keep.

Then a man stood up and said he'd written a poem specially for me. His name was Basil Thorne and he came on stage to read it. It went like this:

Cornwall's mystic and magical charms,
Welcome you Doris with wide open arms,
We need your gift to strengthen those,
Within whose breast, doubts still repose.

163

We wish to know more of the power from within,
That you can receive from our kith and kin,
We believe very strongly and know that it's true,
That Spirit transmits their thoughts through you.

Our gifts are many, varied and free,
All different branches of the very same tree,
We must all make the most of the gifts that we
   have,
And use them to strengthen the weak and the sad.

One thing is certain, we don't always choose,
The right road to take – our gifts best to use,
We hope that your visit will help in some way,
To clarify things for our people today.

And now dear Doris, let's hasten to say,
It's lovely to have you with us today,
We've waited so long so listen we pray,
We hope the next time you come here to stay.

Then he presented me with a copy, all beautifully
written on thick creamy yellow paper. But that wasn't
the end. When Basil left the stage two young girls,
Karen Retallick and Norma Arthur came on to sing me
a song they'd written and composed themselves. It
was a special welcome song and the chorus went:
'Welcome from us Cornish folk to the land of pasties
and cream.'

By the time they finished, my eyes were so full of
tears I could hardly see the stage. I felt quite overwhelmed. The journey had been long and tiring but
the love they'd shown me in St Austell made it worth
every mile.

And just as I was walking out of the hall, a man
leaned over from the audience and said, 'How about
the *Don Lane Show*, Doris?'

I stopped in surprise. The *Don Lane Show* was so
far from my thoughts I felt sure I'd misheard.

'I beg your pardon?'

'The *Don Lane Show*,' the man repeated, 'the last time I saw you Doris was in Australia!'

I couldn't help smiling. What a small world. I'd come all the way to Cornwall to be reminded of the day all the fuss began – when I appeared on the *Don Lane Show* in Australia.

When we got back to our hotel the manageress had seen that the lights were on in the villa, the table was laid up with cold meats and salad and there were hot water bottles warming our beds. It was the perfect end to a perfect evening.

To cap it all, the next morning as we were leaving, the rain actually stopped and the sun came out. The bay was all blue and glistening as we drove away and I could see what looked like little black and white penguins bobbing about in the water.

Penguins? I thought, In Cornwall! But when we got closer they turned out to be little lads in black and white wet suits surfing!

We seemed to spend a lot of time on the road that spring and I dread to think how many miles we covered. We crossed and recrossed from one end of the country to the other and as well as the charity evening in St Austell, I was asked to speak at a literary dinner in Yorkshire.

We drove up and up into the moors until our ears were popping and I hardly dared look out of the window because I'm scared of heights.

'When you said Yorkshire, Laurie,' I said as we passed another sheer drop, 'I thought you meant a town somewhere.'

'So did I,' said Laurie.

But we ended up at a beautiful old world hotel deep in the moors. It was a lovely place, all beams and great log fires and there was time for a nap in our rooms before dinner.

At seven forty-five we went downstairs to the bar where everybody was meeting and we couldn't believe

165

our eyes. The people were crammed in, shoulder to shoulder and extra tables were being carried into the dining-room. How they squeezed so many people in I don't know, but Robbie who drives our Daimler was wedged in so tightly he could only use his left hand! He was able to trap a carrot or two as they went by he told us later, but that was about all!

Johnny Morris was the other guest that night. We'd expected him to tell some animal stories but instead he sang the *Floral Dance* which certainly made a change. You don't associate Johnny Morris with singing.

Then it was my turn. Earlier as I was getting ready I'd heard the name Cocklin and though I didn't know what the literary dinner people were going to make of me, I asked if there was anybody present who knew the name.

'Yes that's me,' called a woman in surprise. 'I'm Mrs Cocklin.'

She was there with her husband who apparently had come with the greatest reluctance.

'Well I'll go for an evening out,' he'd said, 'but it's a load of old balderdash.'

Well I was chatting away to Mrs Cocklin when suddenly a woman's voice interrupted us.

'Oh by the way,' I said, 'I've got a lady here called Lizzie and she wants your husband.'

The man beside her, a little flushed from the wine and the heat all those people had generated, stood up, a bemused expression on his face.

'I just don't believe this. I said to my wife on the way here, if there's any chance of my mother coming back she'd come back, but there isn't. And here you are getting through to her. Nobody ever called her Elizabeth. It was always Lizzie.'

We were under way. A boy called Ashley came back to his mother. Then there was a Mrs Turner.

'Who's Ronnie, living?' I asked.

'Ronnie's my husband,' she said in such a surprised

166

voice I think she suspected Ronnie of passing me a note under the table or something.

It went on and on and it was nearly midnight before we were able to slip away to our room. I'd hardly taken my shoes off though when there was a knock at the door. It was the organizer.

'I'm sorry Mrs Stokes but you're supposed to be signing books. There's a long queue.'

So back I went and signed books till one o'clock in the morning. It was the longest dinner I've ever had!

A month or two later there was another lovely trip in the diary, this time to Portsmouth. Unfortunately I was very tired by the time we got there – but it was my own fault.

The Portsmouth visit happened to coincide with the *Psychic News* dinner dance. Now as a rule, apart from work, John and I hardly ever go out. We do so much travelling and attend so many functions in the line of duty as it were, that we like to spend our free time flopping at home. The last thing we want to do on our nights off is climb into our fancy clothes and go out on the town!

The *Psychic News* dinner dance though is the one exception of the year. It's the chance to meet up with our old friends, have a good gossip and let our hair down if we feel like it and we never miss it. This year in particular was going to be fun I knew, because Russell Grant was going and Derek Jameson was guest of honour and would be making the speech and knowing Derek's sense of humour, it was bound to be hysterical.

Well we had a marvellous time. I danced every dance and we didn't leave till the end, even though we were driving straight down to Portsmouth afterwards. My feet were killing me by the time we came away. It was my own fault entirely, of course, but as I told the audience the next day, when handsome young men come and ask you to dance at my age, you have to get in when you can!

167

Had we been able to set off there and then though, it wouldn't have been too bad, but it was at that point I discovered I'd left my pills behind. My pills are vital. I have to take them every day of my life because my thyroid gland was removed after I was injured by a patient when I was a mental nurse.

For a moment we thought we'd have to go all the way back home to fetch them, but then Laurie had a brainwave.

'Let's call in at the hospital. They'll let you have some, Doris.'

The hospital was just round the corner and they said yes, it would be quite all right, but I would need to see the doctor. So in we went in all our finery, me in my long dress and John in his smart suit and we sat in casualty for half an hour. It was long past midnight by now but we were so exhilarated by the dancing we were wide awake.

At last the doctor called me in.

'Actually I didn't really need to see you,' she confessed, 'but I've heard you on the radio and on TV and I wanted to meet you!' But she organized the drugs for us and at last we were off.

Oh well, I thought, another one and a half hours and we'll be tucked up snug and warm in our hotel. Which just goes to show how wrong you can be even if you're psychic! Not far out of London we came upon a bad accident on the road and we sat there for over an hour while we waited for ambulances and breakdown lorries to clear it up.

Oh dear some poor soul's got it tonight, I thought. You couldn't grumble. You just sat there thankful to be safe.

We eventually got to our hotel at four in the morning. Almost staggering with tiredness John and I let ourselves into our room to be greeted by a great welcoming basket of fruit and a letter addressed to Doris Stokes.

'Heavens above who knows I'm here?' I said to John. 'We're only here two nights.'

But it wasn't a heartrending letter imploring me for

a sitting, it was just a little note from the Chief Accountant thanking me for the books because he'd enjoyed them so much.

As expected we paid for our adventurous night by feeling particularly sluggish when we got up. Well it serves you right, Doris, I told myself. If you will go dancing all night like an eighteen-year-old what do you expect! But as the show drew nearer it stopped being funny.

I just don't know how I'm going to do it, I thought as I went off reluctantly to get ready. But when I started to tune in, in the bathroom as I always do in the hope of a few scraps to get the ball rolling at the theatre, a little boy walked in. He was about ten years old, fairish, and he was wearing a t-shirt with writing across the front.

'Hello, love,' I said drying my face.

'Kittiwick,' said the boy, and, 'Sylvia,' and a bit later, just as he was going, 'Brent.'

I couldn't make out if it was a place or a name but when he vanished I put my head round the bathroom door and called John.

'Can you help me remember, love? It's for tonight. Kittiwick, Sylvia and Brent.'

'Kittiwick, Sylvia and Brent,' repeated John. 'It doesn't sound like much.'

'No I know, but it was a little boy and I bet his Mum's in the audience tonight.'

Driving to the theatre that evening we pulled up at traffic lights and a red car drew alongside us. There were four youngsters inside and when they noticed us, they started shouting 'Hello Doris!' and waving their tickets at us.

The lights changed, the red car shot ahead and suddenly in the back window appeared a big sheet of paper saying:

'We love you, Doris!' and still waving and shouting, the kids led us to the theatre.

After such a warm welcome I was surprised to find the theatre manager a little cool. I couldn't understand it. I'd been to Portsmouth before and everything had gone well then but this particular manager hadn't been there at the time so perhaps he didn't know. Or perhaps he was simply annoyed at having to work on a Sunday. Whatever it was I felt he didn't seem all that pleased to see us.

Fortunately the audience didn't seem to share his feelings. When I walked on stage they didn't just clap, they stamped their feet and cheered. What's more, Sylvia was in the audience and the meaning of the little boy's visit became clear.

Sylvia lived in Kittiwake Close, she'd lost her ten-year-old son, Matthew, and his friend was called Brent. I got Matthew back again when I tuned in and the whole tragic story came out.

Sylvia had been going shopping and Matthew begged to be allowed to stay behind to play with his friend. Some time after his mother had gone, Matthew decided he wanted something from the house, and impulsively tried to climb through one of the small open windows at the top of the main window.

'Oh I was so naughty. So naughty,' said Matthew, repentant now. Somehow he'd slipped with his head caught in the window and broke his neck.

'Mum's not been back home since,' Matthew told me, 'but she's got all my pictures up.'

I didn't understand how this could be, but Sylvia confirmed it was true.

'Oh yes. A friend went and fetched them for me,' she said.

When I came off after the first half the manager was a changed man. He put his arms round me and gave me a big hug.

'That was marvellous,' he said, 'the last time we had anyone like you here it was embarrassing and I thought tonight would be the same, but what a difference. That was marvellous.'

And out came the silver tea service for my intermission cup of tea and everything was all right. I was in.

170

The rest of the evening went just as well. Throughout I'd been rather puzzled because I kept hearing the name Daisy but no one claimed it. Then during question time a little old lady came up to the microphone to ask a question about her sister Maisie.

Instantly I got it.

'That wasn't Daisy, I was getting, it was Maisie!' I exclaimed and immediately Maisie was back.

'I came over with a brain tumour,' she said, 'and now my sister's got the same thing.'

The sister was worried about the suffering she might have to go through but Maisie soothed her fears.

'Don't worry, it's as easy as slipping on butter coming over here,' she assured her, 'and I will be there to take your hand.'

The little old lady's face lit up. 'I'm not worried now. Not if Maisie's with me.'

The other nice surprise was that Joan Scott Alan was in the audience, unknown to me. I'd never met Joan but I'd given a message to her daughter during a demonstration in Nottingham last year. I'd given the daughter Joan's full name, the fact that she nursed the mentally ill and that she wrote beautiful poetry inspired by the spirit people.

Her daughter Pauline was so impressed she phoned her mother the next day and Joan wrote to me enclosing a tape of some of her poems. They were certainly beautiful and I printed one of my favourites in my last book.

Somewhere in the back of my mind I suppose it had registered that Joan lived near Portsmouth but I hadn't heard from her for some time and I never gave her a thought when I walked on the stage. I was absolutely delighted though when a message came through for her and she walked to the microphone and we were able to meet for the first time.

'Joan they're telling me you've retired now from nursing,' I said.

'Yes, Doris, I have.'

171

'But you're still writing the poems.'

Joan smiled. 'Yes I am, in fact I've brought some with me tonight to give to you. There's a special one I've dedicated to you.'

But the spirit people weren't finished.

'They tell me you must concentrate on the poetry but forget the music,' I repeated. It seemed rather a shame because Joan had previously set her poems to music but perhaps she was using vital energy on the music when the important part of her work was the words.

'Oh, I see,' said Joan, perhaps a little disappointed.

Nevertheless afterwards she left me a whole sheaf of poems and as ever they were absolutely beautiful.

This is the one she dedicated to me:

The Interlude

My brief encounter on the earth
Was bitter sweet – I had to search
I could not bear the grief and pain
I knew I'd give but not in vain.

The sacrifice I had to make
To help this soul her path to take
The wretched pain the silent grief
So many souls through her would speak.

I made my journey to the earth
All alone she gave me birth
I clung in love against her breast
In sweet serenity to rest

Her mother love engulfed the air
She washed and tended me with care
No greater love could ever be given
To a tiny soul sent from heaven.

She proudly put me on display
My Gran would laugh – then walk away
You'll spoil that child she would often scold
Mum's reply was a tighter hold.

Her love emitted from her soul
The mother love you can't control
I knew the pain she'd have to bear
When I was taken from her care.

She sang me lullabies at night
I clung to her with all my might.
I knew the interlude was brief
Forgive me Mum – I kiss your feet.

For many months she walked alone
With heavy eyes and heart of stone
Her anguished soul cried out in pain
John Michael please come back again.

Her cries were heard her sorrows shared
The people here did really care
But they all knew that one day soon
The gifts she had would fully bloom.

I met her in her dreams at night
To show her that I was all right
I crept beside her, watched her sleep
Her lovely face made me weep.

Dear Mother I'm so proud of you
All the loving things you do
So many souls you comfort bring
The heavenly choirs for you do sing.

So please may I be forgiven
For leaving you to go to heaven
The Father's works we have to do
And some are the specially chosen few.

When your earthly job is done
You're more than welcome to my home
You'll have the time to stand and stare
And understand just what we shared.

Until that day dear friend, dear mother
I watch and guard you like no other
Your earthly life will always be
A path of love and serenity.

Before I go I feel so sad
For I have not included Dad
The part he plays and love he shares
Is not forgotten over there.

My Mother you will always be
A true companion to me
The love you gave in my interlude
Is being repaid back to you

And now my story has been told
Go in peace till you are old
You have helped the Kingdom come
And I am proud to be your son.

I wish I could tell Joan how much that poem means
to me. I read it over and over again till the tears
streamed down my face. It's the story of the loss of my
baby John Michael, told from John Michael's point of
view and if I can live up to the words of that poem
then I'll be very pleased with myself. Joan has captured
perfectly the way I try to live my life, so that my family
on the other side will not be ashamed of me when I
arrive. I often fail of course but at least I try.

One of my other favourites in the batch she handed
me shows great compassion for the parents of handicapped children:

A Parent's Lament

Ring out the bells
Aloud from the hills
A child is born
Our hearts are filled

With love and pride and joys untold
What perfect beauty to behold

We watch her grow
With hearts so full
Of love and caring
But she's no fool

The moment we both creep away
From that nice cradle where she lay
A cry rings out

An icy hand grips both our hearts
That cry is something quite apart
A different ring – what can it be?
Our little child is almost three

We watch her play
Why can't she walk?
All other children seem to talk.

With heavy hearts we take advice
And find this soul will pay the price
For we are told in gentle tones
This child can never be left alone.

Oh God our hearts cry out in pain
What did we do to upset you
That we should rear a child in vain?

The dear Lord heard our cry and said
Hush now, take your child to bed
Then listen to what I say – let me explain
These children are my precious gifts
It's not meant to bring you pain.

If you just stop and think it through
My special gift I've sent to you
To teach you simple things of life
And most of all she's saved from strife.

The world is such a greedy place
Where man fights man
And hate meets hate.

Our worldly goods we proudly show
But when we pass where do they go?
To be passed down?
And so it goes
NO that is mine NOT for Aunt Rose.

Have you heard all this before?
Well now I knock upon your door

My special gift to you I give
That you may learn from her to live.

A life that's full and very sweet
With face upturned sat at your feet
With love that melts the hardest heart
Take this child set apart
Watch her try to talk and sing
And then, thank God for everything.

Jean's poems are always a great joy to read and they
brought a lovely evening to a close for me. As the
demonstration ended the audience went mad. There
was so much clapping and stamping and waving of

handkerchiefs they almost pulled me off the stage. I looked up at the swaying rows of cheering faces, all 2,000 of them, and it didn't matter how fagged out I'd been earlier I knew I was doing the right thing. I was on the right track, doing the work I'd been made for.

Chapter Twelve

I couldn't believe my eyes when I opened the paper. BATTLE OF THE PSYCHIC SUPERSTARS said the giant headline strung across two pages and beneath it was a report of demonstrations given by myself and medium Doris Collins as if we were arch rivals fighting for supremacy.

It was annoying because it's so untrue. Doris Collins and I have known each other for years. We once even shared the *Psychic News* award for Spiritualist of the Year. Doris is a very good medium and I respect her. Our styles are different just as any two people working in the same field will bring their own different personalities to the job, but there's certainly no need for us to 'battle'. There's more than enough work around to keep us, and goodness knows how many other mediums as well, fully occupied for the rest of our lives.

More than anything the story was a disappointment. The reporter had come along to a public meeting at Fairfield Halls, Croydon and we'd had some marvellous evidence. I got two lots of twins back including a pair who'd gone over after a premature birth. The poor mother had gone into labour unexpectedly on holiday in Greece and she'd lost both babies.

'You're grieving, love, because you left them in Greece,' I said. 'You came home and you left your babies there.'

'That's right,' she sobbed.

'Well, you didn't leave them, love, because they're here with you now. Two little girls and I'm getting the names Amy and Donna.'

'That's what I called them!' she cried and her whole face became radiant.

Not long afterwards I heard the name Stephen.

'I want a little boy named Stephen,' I said. 'Our side of life.'

And to my surprise a little boy, no more than eight or nine years old came racing down to the stage.

'I'm Stephen,' he cried, while behind him, his mother struggled to catch up.

It was a young man I was talking to and since the woman didn't look old enough to have a grown up son I felt sure it must be Stephen's father.

'It's a man's voice, love,' I told her, 'a young voice.'

'Yes, that's right. I lost my husband when Stephen was only six months old,' she said.

'Does my Daddy know me, does my Daddy know I'm here?' asked Stephen bouncing up and down.

'Yes he does, darling,' I assured him and to prove it his father said, 'Tell him I know about Simon. He's a big bully.'

'Yes he is,' Stephen agreed. 'Actually he gave me a black eye last week.'

'Well stand up to him, son,' said his father, 'and if you can't hit him, kick him. You only have to stand up to a bully once.'

Stephen stood there taking it all in, his head on one side. He was a dear little soul, very old-fashioned and well spoken.

'He likes Tim, though,' the father went on.

'Do you know a Timothy?' I asked. 'Your father says you get on well with him.'

'Oh yes he's a good chap,' said Stephen.

Then the father began to talk about other members of the family. He mentioned Kitty, but before Stephen's mother could answer Stephen jumped in again. 'He's talking about Auntie Kit, Mummy.'

'Kitty's very good to him,' said the father.

'Well actually I don't see her very often,' said Stephen 'but when I do see her she's very good to me.'

At the end of the message I said to Stephen, 'Because it's a very special occasion because you've never seen your Daddy, I'm going to give you the big centre piece of flowers to take home. Your Daddy tells me your Mummy's got a car so she'll be able to manage it.'

So Stephen came up on to the stage and staggered off with the flower arrangement that was nearly as big as he was.

I thought that was last I'd seen of Stephen but after the demonstration was finished, when I was relaxing in the dressing-room, there came a knock on the door. It was Stephen bringing me a single flower from the spray.

'This is to tell you I love you,' he said.

I put my arms round him. 'And I love you too,' I said. And suddenly there was a great flash and I looked up to find the photographer for the newspaper was still there, taking pictures.

'There's a photographer taking pictures of us,' Stephen whispered.

'Yes I know,' I said, 'we're going to be in the *Sunday Mirror*.'

Stephen's eyes widened. 'Oh really. Are we? How spiffing!'

He was thrilled by the idea and so looking forward to the day the paper came out. I too waited eagerly to see the pictures of the two of us and the single flower.

But when the day came there was no mention of Stephen and no photograph. Instead just this battle of the psychic superstars nonsense. It was such a shame and I could imagine how disappointed Stephen must have been.

Mind you, to be fair, the newspapers are mostly very kind to me and I've had some lovely write ups. It's odd to see yourself as others see you and some of the descriptions make me laugh. John Slim from the *Birmingham Evening Post*, was very nice and he had an amusing turn of phrase . . .

'She emits a sudden, chesty laugh which hits her hotel room like a quick half hundred weight of bucketed gravel . . .' he wrote, 'Doris Stokes . . . is a motherly mixture of humility and good humour who carries her ample poundage with the implacability of a benevolent battleship . . .'

John and I were in stitches over that one.

'When people start describing you as a battleship, it really is time to go on a diet!' I sighed.

One interview I'd been anxious about was with Jean Rook of the *Daily Express*. She'd seemed very friendly on the phone but I'd heard she can be very sharp about people in print, and I couldn't imagine what she'd say about me. If you wanted to I suppose it would be quite easy to do a mickey-taking piece about spooks and ghosties.

Jean had a very tight schedule and what with one thing and another she ended up coming to interview me in my hospital bed. I'd had to go into hospital for a couple of days for tests – as I have to regularly since I had cancer and Jean obviously didn't think much of my chances because she wrote afterwards . . .

'Mrs Stokes was lying in bed, pale as her cream satin négligée. And looking too close for my comfort to the Threshold she professes to cross as casually as most of us move from room to room.'

The one thing Jean didn't want was a sitting. She put up a great barrier and was most emphatic that she didn't want to talk to anyone. It was strictly an interview. Nevertheless she was a great friend of Diana Dors and while she was there Diana popped in.

'Jean's very good at tennis you know,' she said.

That shook Jean a bit I think. It turned out that Diana had never known Jean played tennis and in fact has become so keen on the game that she's having a tennis court built at her home.

After that I stuck mainly to the questions, but sometimes things happened that I couldn't help. Jean stayed a long time and she even waited while I went off for one particular test. On the way back to the ward I sensed Diana with me.

'Oh Di – could you go and look at the results for

me?' I asked because this was the test I'd been worried about.

She zipped off and a few moments later she was back. 'It's all right, kid. You're clear,' she said.

Back in my room I smiled at Jean. 'It's all right. I can relax and have a cup of tea now. I'm clear. Diana's just told me.'

Jean looked rather doubtful and made no comment but later on the doctor looked in.

'It's all right, doctor, I know the results already,' I told him cheerfully, 'I'm clear.'

He grinned. 'Yes you are.'

Then just as she was leaving, I did it again. Earlier I'd heard the name Eileen, and it came back suddenly connected with a man who passed very quickly with a heart attack.

It meant nothing to Jean, but the photographer turned pale.

'My mother's name is Eileen and my father died of a heart attack seven months ago,' he said shakily.

'Well tell your Mum your Dad's fine now, love,' I told him.

After that I couldn't think what Jean would write and I was a bit jittery until the paper came out. But I needn't have worried.

This is what she wrote:

Medium rare

I make a pig's ear of it when the spirits are all trying to talk to me at once, says Doris Stokes

Even for sceptics, Mrs Doris Stokes is the ultimate psychic phenomenon.

Few people in this world – even with one foot in the next – can pack the London Palladium with its capacity

2,000 audience, plus standing room. And not a dry eye in the sobbing, cheering, rapturous house.

Mrs Stokes is a built-in telephone exchange to the Other World. She claims to speak to the dead. She plugs them in to their living relatives. Takes messages from the Great Unknown like an answering service.

For grieving multitudes, this 65-year-old spiritualist is the antidote to death's sting. She is Victory, in a £100 beaded evening dress, over the grave.

Whether or not you believe a word she claims the dead tell her, her delivery is stunning. She dismisses all candlelit hocus and gloomy pocus. All the audience gets is a well-lit, plump, grey, permed housewife, talking on an imaginary phone to their loved ones who are not lost.

She gives the distraught parents of a 17-year-old, who died of a heart attack, all the chat they want to hear: – 'Change that coloured photograph you keep of him, lovey – he doesn't like it, he says his hair doesn't look right.'

Stokes is the thoroughly modern medium. She will appear for three Sunday Nights at the Palladium this summer – already sold out.

Comfort

Even Frankie Goes to Hollywood causes no more stampede for tickets than Doris Goes to the Other Side and Back.

When we met last week in London's Guy's Hospital for a rare 'private sitting', Mrs Stokes was lying in bed, pale as her cream satin negligee. And looking too close for my comfort to the Threshold she professes to cross as casually as most of us move from room to room.

She has survived 13 cancer operations. 'When I told Dick Emery I'd lost a breast, my thyroid, my womb, a large chunk of intestine and my right ovary, he joked: "Doris, they want you over the Other Side but you've too much work to do so they're taking you across bit by bit".'

She added: 'I'm not worried about today's tests. I took Diana Dors down to the X-ray unit with me, and she's already checked on the results and told me I'm clear. So we can have a ciggy now, and relax,' she said, lighting her Menthol.

Did Mrs Stokes know it was the eve of the anniversary of Diana Dors' own death from cancer? (my first slip – don't feed the medium information). Did she know I'd come to ask her to raise Diana (slip two – don't show the medium your hand and give her something to grasp at).

Right out of the blue she claims is heaven, Mrs Stokes fixed me with her unnaturally huge, cloud-grey eyes and said: 'Diana says you're a terrifically good tennis player.'

Diana, though the closest friend in life, didn't even know I played tennis. And nobody but my family and the building firm knows I've just paid a deposit on a hard tennis court.

Game to Miss Dors and Mrs Stokes.

May I see Diana? 'No and I can't,' said the clairaudient (as opposed to voyant) who can only hear the dead. 'I can hear her in this room as clearly as the evening she died, when I didn't even know she was in hospital.'

How did Di take the news of her death?

'She was angry when she first got there, like Noele Gordon two weeks ago – they'd fought so hard to stay down here. Diana was angry too when Alan committed suicide (Diana Dors's husband Alan Lake shot himself five months after her death).

Laughed

'They came together to me and she told me how he did it – put the shotgun between his knees and balanced it under his chin. She kept saying: "How could you leave our baby? (their son Jason, now 16). Why didn't you have the guts to stay with him?" You know how straight out with everything she was.

184

'When he told her "I was like a bird without wings without you it was hopeless," she forgave him everything.'

What do you wear on the Other Side? 'Anything you fancy. You certainly don't wear wings or a white sheet and go "oooh!" and frighten folk to death.'

'To WHAT?' I said cunningly. A slip of the psyche, laughed this Grantham-born daughter of a Romany who 'lived across the road from the Prime Minister.'

'Margaret got awfully upset one night because she heard some kids outside church whisper: "There goes Creeping Jesus" – she thought they meant her Dad, who was a lay preacher. I told her not to worry, as they meant me.

'I worried though. I tried to hide what I could hear *and* see – because when I was young I could do both. I can still see spirit children – because I've lost four and love them so much.'

When her longest surviving child, John Michael, died at five months, she and her healer husband, John, accepted her unwanted gift. 'I really DIDN'T want to know, I wanted to be normal and ordinary. Sometimes I still tell the spirits to "push off" if they start whispering to me at a party.'

Do the blue lights which is all she can see of the spirits flickering above her audience, ever glow angry?

'Oh, they do, dear, they tell me to "get on with it, woman" when I get my wires crossed, and I do make mistakes when they're all trying to talk at once,' said the psychic whose greatest strength is admitting weakness, even to desperate parents, with: 'No, I'm guessing. Don't take that. I'm making a pig's ear, don't believe what I'm saying.'

'And they sometimes get cross with This Side. The nastiest case I had was a widow all in black, sobbing "that's my husband Jim, he only passed over last week." and Jim yelling in my other ear: "The bloody hypocrite, she's sitting next to the boyfriend she was carrying on with when I was in hospital." '

Chatting

Six years ago, she began to raise huge audiences from her soirees with the spirits and massive money from her four autobiographical books. 'I like the money. I just bought a new house,' she said.

I grabbed at her grasping flesh. Nothing materialized but a modest £50,000 semi-detached.

Her much talked-about limousine is hired: 'Because I have to stretch out my body to ease the pains.' Her £1,000 cut of an expensively staged Evening with Doris Stokes goes to charity.

'Who's Pepe?' she said. 'There's a dog barking!' 'Peri,' I said. My long-lost poodle, dead 15 years. 'No not dead, dear, jumping about all over the place.'

She had now been chatting, almost non-stop, for two hours. And not always to me and the photographer, alone with her in the room.

'Who's Eileen?' she'd asked, an hour before. Now she said: 'I've got someone here who died very suddenly of a heart attack. He's connected with the Eileen I asked about earlier.'

My photographer, Barry Gomer's father, died of a heart attack seven months ago. His mother's name is Eileen. Even I didn't know until 10 minutes before we left the office, which photographer would be going with me. Or his mother's name.

'Well, tell your mother he's fine, lovely,' she said There was a long silence. For startled Barry it wasn't dead.

My spirits sank. Which is where I intended them to remain. 'You've a barrier built up against me, lovey,' said the woman who, in one of her rare sightings, alleges she watched Tommy Cooper rise from his body when he slumped, dying, on live TV.

I have an electrified fence, I thought silently (maybe she reads your mind, like a palm). When my beloved father died, 16 years ago, he made me swear on everything but the Bible I'd never try to contact him.

'Why do I get a conservatory?' she suddenly said.

She knew she'd cracked it. How many journalists have a 'conservatory' as opposed to a greenhouse, or cloche?

And why did my mother pick this week, after 40 years in our Yorkshire family home, to have my father's treasured, but now disintegrating Victorian conservatory restored?

'I'm sure I could make contact at a sitting at home,' beamed Mrs Stokes, now lit up like the sun shining through glass, brightly. 'But I'm only the bridge, I can't do it if you're not willing and he's not willing.'

'We're not,' I said, speaking up before Pa weakened and had a word with Mrs Stokes.

I'd prefer to speak to him quietly, myself. And much as I still adore him, at some later date.

Daily Express
Monday May 6 1985

Yes, generally I can't complain. The papers have been very fair with me. Only one article has made me really angry and that wasn't about me at all. It was about Diana Dors and Alan Lake. It was a very nasty piece full of insinuations that Diana and Alan didn't love each other. That Alan was off with other women and Diana was having an affair in the last year of her life.

I was furious when I read it. How could they say such terrible things about two lovely people who weren't here to defend themselves. And what about Jason? Hadn't he suffered enough without reading such terrible things about his parents?

The more I thought about it the angrier I became. I couldn't believe it. Diana was far too ill in the last year of her life to be interested in an affair and as for Alan – he was a flirt, that's the way he was made, but he didn't mean anything by it. He worshipped Diana.

I got so upset by the whole thing that I couldn't eat

for two days and in the end Ramanov gave me a talking to.

'Child, this won't do,' he said sternly. 'You are wasting your energy and making yourself ill. You have work to do and others that depend on you.'

He was right, of course, but then Ramanov always is.

He has been spending quite a lot of time with me lately. We've been going through a difficult patch with Terry and though the crowds wouldn't think it from my smiling face on stage, life at home has been very hard at times.

Last year Terry had a dreadful accident. He could have been killed but he was lucky and escaped with severe concussion. He seemed to get over it very well, but then just after Christmas he began to look ill. He developed violent headaches, he had no energy and suddenly for no reason, he'd fly into terrible tempers.

There were quite a few unhappy scenes at home before we discovered the problem. The shock of the accident had brought on sugar diabetes and his body was completely out of balance. In the meantime though, my nerves got very bad and I sometimes fled to my room in tears. But I wasn't alone. Ramanov was always there.

'Why does this have to happen now?' I sobbed one night. 'Just when everything's lovely and we've got this beautiful house. Why does it have to be spoiled?'

'I never promised you sunshine all the way did I?' said Ramanov. 'Learn from it. There are many lessons here.'

Well I tried and I think I've learned to be more tolerant. I've tried to understand why Terry gets these violent moods and bit by bit we've guided him through. As long as he sticks to his diet he should be all right.

I don't want it to sound as if Ramanov runs my life for me because he doesn't. The spirit world won't do that. If you have a problem you have to try to solve it yourself, but if you've tried everything you can think of and nothing's worked, then a prayer to the spirit world will usually be answered.

Many times I've turned to Ramanov in despair and said it's no good, I've tried and tried and I'm at my wits' end. Can you help? And the next morning I've woken up with a new idea in my mind that turns out to be the solution to the problem. But you do have to help yourself. It's no good saying 'I need £1,000. Please God work a miracle.' They will only help if they can see you've genuinely done your best.

Mind you, although he doesn't run my life, Ramanov certainly lets me know if I'm straying from the path. If I start to get too materialistic he steers me back and shows me where I'm going wrong.

Now I have got a little money for the first time in my life it would be so easy to go wrong. I used to be a great idealist. I used to say that material things don't matter – and they don't really – but in spite of that, it is nice to have a beautiful bedroom to relax in and a lovely house to come home to and I'm not going to pretend it's not.

I'd be telling a lie if I didn't say it's nice to have a house with nice gardens and to be able to look out of the window and say this belongs to us.

People at the mobile home park say they can't understand it. Why on earth are we saddling ourselves with all this at our ages. But I say, you've already had it love. You've had your beautiful house, you know what it's like. I never have. I've always lived in ex-servicemen's flats or prefabs or rented houses where I've had to ask permission to hold sittings or have people in. Now I can do what I like. Maybe it's late in life but at least I can say I've done it.

One thing I thought was lovely was that when the article about my house appeared in *Woman's Own*, I didn't have one letter begrudging my good fortune. Everybody wrote to say how beautiful it was and that I deserved it. I think I do too! I've worked very hard

189

and I've known what it's like not to have two pennies to rub together. I think I deserve a little comfort now.

Of course it's no good being the richest body in the cemetery, as Ramanov keeps reminding me, so I do a lot of charity appearances and give away as much as I can and it gives me great pleasure to do so. It's so nice to be able to help people out in a practical way at last.

I do get tired and fed up with work at times and wonder if I'm mad gallivanting around the country at my age, but Ramanov finds lessons for me in the smallest things.

One day in early spring the builders cleared away a pile of rubbish beside the drive of our house and when I went to look I saw a group of tiny crocuses that had been buried by the bricks. They were bruised and battered but they'd struggled up through all the rubbish and were flowering bravely. And as I admired them I heard Ramanov's voice in my ear.

'See what I've been telling you for so long,' he said. 'As long as you keep the spark alive, no matter how bruised and battered you may be you can survive, just as these fragile little flowers have managed to struggle through the bricks to give beauty to the world.'

His words often come back to me when I'm moaning about being tired, and also when I'm talking to someone who is stricken by grief. The human spirit is battered and bruised by grief just as the crocuses were battered by bricks, yet if we can just keep that spark of love alive we'll come through it. And you know grief isn't a bad thing. It's God's healing gift to us, because it enables us to cry. Without crying the bitterness would stay inside and make you ill.

I know it's easy for me to say, but truly no one can escape grief – not even a medium who knows that loved ones live on and talks to them every day. The tears flow because you can't touch them any more. It's the physical presence we miss.

Although I know with certainty that there's another world, if anything happened to John I would go through exactly the same thing. I would weep and weep because I couldn't put my arms round him any more. That's grief and nobody can bear that cross for us. But if we know that God or our guide is there to hold our hand, we can get through it.

Ramanov comes along at the most unlikely moments. On May 8th 1985 we were celebrating the 40th anniversary of VE day and it was an extra special occasion for John and I because it was also the day he came home from the prisoner-of-war camp. He got a beautiful new leather jacket out of that!

Anyway there we were toasting each other in tea, when Ramanov interrupted.

'This is all very well,' he said, 'but while you are celebrating peace, there are wars going on all over the world. Until you learn to live as brothers and love one another you won't have peace.'

It made me stop and think. I mean people are always saying, if there is a spirit world why don't they do more to stop wars and violence, but my Mum and Dad couldn't run the country when they lived here, so why should they be able to run the country now, just because they've been to the spirit world. And after all, it's the people here now, who're making wars.

As Ramanov's said before. 'God gave you a beautiful world to live in and look what you're doing with it.'

It's no good us complaining. We've made the problems and we must solve them.

When I came back from St Austell I brought a poster with me which reads: 'Any act of kindness no matter how small, is never wasted!' and I've got it up on my wall. It's so true. If everyone followed that advice, the small acts of kindness would lead to greater acts of kindness and we'd be well on the way towards loving each other.

I know that it is true – just as the reverse is true. Small acts of unkindness can have a ripple effect and do far more damage than the original mean act.

I remember doing a demonstration at SAGB not long

ago and as soon as I walked onto the stage I could feel there was something wrong. Well it was a terrible night. I gave the wrong messages to the wrong people and I couldn't understand it. I've not had a night as bad as that for years.

This happened about the time we were having difficulty with Terry and I wondered if the traumas at home might be affecting me. Whatever it was, I knew I'd been dreadful and I apologized to the people there. They were very sweet and said it was fine, but I knew they were just being kind. It was not fine and I knew it.

Then two days later I had a note from a woman who'd been in the audience. She said how sorry she was that I was unhappy with the evening. We weren't hostile to you, it was the man on the door, she said. Apparently the doors had opened at five-forty-five even though the demonstration didn't start till seven and this man was shouting at people and telling them to shut-up and refusing to let them leave their seats to go to the loo or get a drink. Naturally they didn't like it, the hostility and anger built up and the evening was spoiled for everyone.

That one small act of unkindness ruined things for over one hundred and fifty people and many of them probably lost the chance of making contact with loved ones – a chance they'd been waiting for for months.

I've been doing a lot of public demonstrations lately and at most of them, I'm happy to say, the atmosphere's been marvellous. It makes such a difference. It's the love in the air that brings the spirit people close and the more love that's generated, the more contacts we get.

Some extraordinary things have come through. One night at Woolwich I was talking to a mother on the other side who was trying to comfort her husband and daughter who were grief stricken. She gave me a number of names and family details and then the daughter explained how they came to be attending the meeting that night.

Her mother had been to see me last year at a demonstration in London and had obviously been impressed.

'The Saturday before she died, she said if I'm going to come back through anybody it will be Doris Stokes,' said the daughter. 'She made me promise to buy tickets for this show and to come with Dad.'

'We bought the tickets for her,' said the bemused father, 'and she's come.'

On a lighter note, I was talking to a young boy who'd been killed in an accident. He was chatting away to his sister who was quite happy and regarded it all as perfectly natural.

'And there was a Mr Barns or Burns,' said the boy, 'he was a right pig.'

The sister laughed, 'Oh that'll be the coroner. Yes he was!'

But his next words were drowned out by the squawking of a parrot.

'Good boy Joey. Good boy Joey. Who's a pretty boy then?' it screeched and I couldn't hear a word anybody else was saying.

'Could you keep the parrot quite a minute?' I begged the spirit people. Then I turned to the audience.

'Does anyone recognize a parrot called Joey?'

A young girl came forward at once. 'It's my mother's parrot.'

'Well she's brought it back with her, love.'

'Have a Guinness, have a Guinness,' muttered the parrot into my ear and I burst out laughing.

'Oh they never taught him to say that! He's saying have Guinness, have a Guinness!'

The girl nodded. 'That's right. Dad used to come in drunk and that's what the parrot would say.'

The audience, of course, loved it.

I must say my theatre visits have been much more enjoyable for me lately because of a marvellous shop I

193

heard about in Forest Hill, London. Some years ago, as I tell everybody, I had a masectomy and until you have something like that you don't realize the problems it causes.

For instance, you're like a bird with one wing, particularly when you're my size and it's very easy to over balance if you're not careful because your weight is no longer evenly distributed. You have to think twice about all kinds of everyday things, like climbing into the bath. Climb in from the wrong side and you're likely to go flying – as I did a few months ago. To make matters worse we didn't have any grab bars on the sides of our bath, so I couldn't get out again. I just lay there with my legs in the air not sure whether to laugh or cry!

Going on stage was another problem. The false boob they'd given me at the hospital weighed a ton and was very hot to wear, particularly under spotlights. When I got home my muscles would be aching and I found I'd perspired so much it was soaking wet.

I'd more or less resigned myself to the fact that I'd got to learn to live with it, when someone told me about this girl in Forest Hill who was going to have to close down her shop because she couldn't make a living wage. Apparently she stocked special bras for ladies like me and she has special lambswool pads to go inside them.

She sounded just the person I was looking for and I discovered she runs a wonderful service as well. Sometimes she tries on as many as seventy bras to make sure she gets the fit absolutely right. She measured every little part of me and if it fitted in one place and not another, she'd take it off and try another. She spent ages, altering a piece here and a piece there. What a difference from the hospital where they simply put a tape measure round you and give you a bra, a bag and a piece of foam filled stuff to put inside, and that's it.

What's more this girl doesn't charge for the service,

only for the articles she sells. And when any of her ladies are going to a wedding or a special function, they take all their clothes to the shop, dress, shoes and everything and they try it all on with the bra to make sure it looks right.

Now that's what I call doing God's work and it'll be a tragedy if she has to give it up for lack of money.

Chapter Thirteen

'Doris,' said the young man at the microphone, 'just before my grandad died seven years ago, we had a blazing row. I told him to drop dead. And he did. It's been playing on my mind ever since. Do you think he blames me?'

It was question time. The short spot that opens the second half of my public demonstrations, and this lad had obviously been waiting all evening to ask the question that had been worrying him for seven years.

'Oh you poor soul,' I said. 'Of course he wouldn't blame you. He wouldn't bear any malice. We all say it when we're young don't we. He's just come through and he says, "I was a bit of a nagger." But he's watched over you ever since and he says you've been right down on the floor and he's picked you up and you're doing all right now. That row doesn't make a bit of difference. He still loves you.'

I get asked all sorts of things at question time but the same subjects do occur again and again, so I thought it might be helpful to collect a few examples of questions and answers from recent demonstrations. These are the sort of things people want to know:

Q. My friend's still got her Dad's ashes and she doesn't know where she should put them. What should she do?

A. We've been asked some rum things before! He says, 'I don't care a damn, love, I'm here.' If it'll make you happy I think he liked rivers, you could spread them on water. But let him go free with love and he will come back with love.

196

Q. My question is about senility. If people are senile before they pass, do they remember what happened to them when they get to the other side?

A. No, because they are not responsible for their actions. When they get to the other side they go into hospital and are nursed back with love. They don't remember the details of their passing. When they come back they usually say: 'I got very difficult towards the end.'

Q. If a murderer goes on to a different plane on the other side what happens to someone who commits suicide?

A. They are sick in the mind so they go into a special hospital where they are nursed until they're well. The person you're talking about was in a car wasn't he love?

Q. Yes

A. He's here and he just told me: 'I was in the car under some trees and I was found,' he said. He'd had words with someone and wanted to frighten them.

A. Well he's here now love and he's better. He's fine now. He's not in hellfire or anything like that.

Q. My little girl died when she was two. Who looks after her? Does she still play?

A. Yes. She's happy, love. They don't let anything hurt the spirit children. They even keep them away from our grief. A spirit mother looks after them. You have a grandmother over there and she is looking after your little girl. When there are no close relatives on the other side a girl who's gone over without knowing the joys of motherhood will be given the child to look after.

Q. Is it possible to see someone if they have died? I did several times and I was told I was imagining it. I think I upset him because I told him I couldn't take any more and I haven't seen him since. Did I do the wrong thing?

A. If it was wrong, love, they'd have left me years ago because when I was young I used to get so fed up with the spirit people I used to say, oh push off – leave me alone. I think they are giving you time to adjust and if you have psychic ability you must use it, love. If it happens again say: Hello, how are you doing?

Q. My friend lost her husband in 1983. He died from a rare disease. Now they want to open him up. Is it the right thing to do?

A. He's just come in. I think it was something to do with the brain wasn't it because he says, 'I went like a baby'.

Q. Yes that's right.

A. He says it doesn't matter a bit what they do with his body and if it will help someone else let them get on with it.

Q. I lost my little boy about two years ago. I moved from that flat but people say the little girl who moved in keeps pointing when there's nothing there and things are being moved. Could it be my little boy?

A. Yes. The little girl will see him. Children are psychic until ten or eleven. He just wanders in and out to see what's happening in his old home.

Q. Last year my sister went over. Just before she died she had a row with my brother and we wonder whether she's forgiven him.

A. Of course she has. She went very tragically, very quickly didn't she? It was a virus and it was all over in 48 hours she tells me. Don't cry she says because she's all right and of course she doesn't bear any malice. We all fall out now and then but it doesn't mean anything.

Q. You seem to pick up people who haven't passed long ago. Does that mean it's harder for people to come back if they passed a long time ago?

A. It's not harder love it's just that when someone has just passed their relatives are still grieving and they want to reassure them. They stay close to comfort them. But the other night I had a girl whose mother passed over when she was three and she came back to talk to her daughter twenty-seven years on!

Q. If you carry a kidney donor card and leave parts of your body to someone on earth, does it hinder your progression into spirit?

A. Oh no, love. Blimey I hope they've got my parts parcelled and labelled! I've had so many bits and pieces taken away, love. Whether I'll be any good to anyone now I don't know but John and I have put in our will that anything that can be used, can be used. It doesn't make any difference to us over there. My mother only had one eye. She lost it at birth but when I saw my mother on the other side I couldn't understand what was different about her at first — then I realized she had two eyes.
They can put me in the dustbin when I've gone for all the difference it'll make to me. I'll be away.

Q. You never seem to talk to foreign people in public meetings why's that?

A. I do. The other night I had a woman from Cyprus, but I agree I talk to more British people in public demonstrations. I think it's because I have trouble getting my name round foreign names and it takes up so much time, it's better to save them for private sittings when I have longer.

Q. If a child is not born on earth what age does it grow up to in the spirit world?

A. The age it should have been had it lived here. It will grow up and be brought back to see its mother and when she goes over she will recognize him or her immediately, even though she never saw her child on earth.

Q. If you lose a baby what happens when the person looking after it gets too old to look after it?
A. They don't, love. There's always someone there to take care of them and when you've reached the age you were meant to reach you don't grow any older.

Q. I was waiting to adopt a baby when my nan passed over. Does she know I've got my son now?
A. Of course she does. She comes to see you regularly.

Q. The evening my grandmother died I was in the bedroom and she said there was someone else in the room and she didn't want them there. Who was it?
A. Someone from the spirit world come to get her. The minute you see that you know you're about to pop your clogs! Your gran probably would say take him away, because she didn't want to go just then.

Q. If you have more than one husband, who do you end up with?
A. If you loved them both equally you'd go to both because there is no jealousy. But if you didn't get on on earth you probably wouldn't want to see each other again so you wouldn't. You go where the love is.

Q. How do you develop psychic power?
A. Everyone has a psychic spark but in some it's stronger than in others. Sometimes it is inherited and sometimes you get interested in psychic things and it just happens. Join a good developing circle – you'll hear of one through your nearest spiritualist church. Or if that doesn't suit you sit with two or

three friends in love and harmony and offer yourself in service.

Q. If you have an animal put down, are you held
responsible even if it was for the good of the
animal?

A. No, love. I hope someone would do the same for
me if I was suffering and never going to get well.
But animals live on too and they are fit and healthy
on the other side. You will meet your pets again.

Q. Do they celebrate birthdays on the other side.

A. Yes. They are lucky. They have two celebrations,
the day they were born on earth and the day they
arrived in the spirit world.

Q. Can I put in a request now to work with animals
over there?

A. Oh yes, love. There are always poor animals that
are put down because they're unwanted or are
killed in accidents and they are nursed back on the
other side too. They tell me you've got a dog called
Sammy now.

Q. Yes and I love him to bits!

Q. If they watch you from the other side, do they come
into the room or do they watch you from somewhere else?

A. Are you worried about your privacy, love? There
wouldn't be any babies born if everyone thought
like that. No, they respect our privacy. They come
when you send out love. If you think, isn't this
lovely I wish so and so could be here to see it – they
come.

Q. If we are all here to learn, what have the people in
Ethiopia got to learn?

A. I'm afraid I can't answer that, love. I've often
wondered myself. It's the people at the top who're

to blame. But the rest of us can learn from the suffering people in Ethiopia. Look at Bob Geldoff. He went there and was touched by what he saw. It will have changed him for the better.

Q. Have we all got a spirit guide?

A. Yes, every single one of us. Someone on the other side volunteers to give up their progression in the spirit world to guide us even before our bodies are conceived. They are waiting and our spirit is waiting to come to earth and when we go back the guide goes back. You might call it your conscience or your instinct or a hunch, but it is your spirit guide trying to lead you onto the right path.

Q. I lost my daughter last year and I want to know if I live to be ninety, will she still be there when I go over or will she have gone on?

A. No darling it takes hundreds of years. It doesn't matter how old you are she'll still know you are her mother. It doesn't matter how long we have to wait, we'll see our kids again. The love link is eternal.

Q. I have been grieving badly for eleven months now and I wonder if that grief will stop the person from progressing in the spirit world?

A. Well yes, I'm sorry to say it'll make it more difficult. You have to let them go free with love so that they can come back with love. We all have to go through a grieving period, but it makes them sad to see us unhappy.

Q. Is healing hereditary?

A. Well I inherited my gift from my father who was a Romany Gypsy so I should think healing might be inherited too. You only have to want to help people and if the gift is there, it will come.

Q. My mum didn't have a very happy life but I have a very very happy life and I want to share it with her a bit more but I'm frightened.

A. Well it scared me at first, love, but really there's nothing to be afraid of. It's as natural as breathing. Your mum will be close to you, just say hello to her and put a flower by her picture with your love.

Q. I lost five relatives recently and I wonder if they are together. Also does it hurt my dad because I love him so much?

A. They will be together and it hurts your dad to see you unhappy. You can't live with your daddy in the spirit world can you, love? You've got your own life to lead and your own family to think of. You mustn't send all your love with your daddy. He's happy in his new life but your grief is making him sad.

As you can see, the questions come in all shapes and sizes and every question time is slightly different but these are the types of questions I'm most often asked. Perhaps yours is amongst them.

Chapter Fourteen

The other day I was going through the mail as I do first thing every morning when I shook one envelope and out fell a faded snapshot. People often send me pictures of their spirit children for my wall, but I knew immediately that this was something different. It was old and blurry, not a bit like the glossy colour photographs we take today.

Curiously I picked up the magnifying glass to have a good look and suddenly the face of my dear old Mum leapt out at me. I gazed at the picture in delight. It showed three ladies dressed in the style of the twenties or thirties walking along a street in Skegness and I knew them all; Winifred Webb, Florrie Hodson and Mum. Mum and two of her friends were obviously enjoying a holiday, or possibly a day trip at our nearest seaside resort.

People often ask me why I've printed pictures of my father in previous books but not my mother. Well it's not that I loved mum any less – it's just that there are hardly any pictures of her in existence. You see Mum had only one eye, she lost the other at birth during a forceps delivery and she went through life wearing an ugly old shade. She was always a bit self conscious of it and consequently when anyone got a camera out, Mum would head off in the opposite direction. She was extremely reluctant to have her picture taken to say the least and now there are hardly any photographs to remind us of her. That's why I was so thrilled to receive the Skegness snapshot and since then we've had it blown up and I've included it in this book.

You can tell just by looking at the way Mum's hat is pulled down low on her forehead how much she hated that eye shade and tried to hide it. Yet when I saw her in the spirit world she had two eyes, good as new. We lose all our infirmities over there and Mum had got rid of that patch for good.

Memories of my family have been crowding in lately because I've just come back from Lincoln which is very nearly home ground. Actually it should have been home ground proper, but we had such difficulty over the arrangements for a demonstration at Grantham that we moved the whole thing down the road to Lincoln. I mentioned earlier the trouble there was over ticket touts and some people getting twenty tickets while others had none. Well in the end there was so much bad feeling I felt I couldn't work in that sort of atmosphere, so we laid on coaches and ferried all those who wanted to go to Lincoln and back, and the proceeds of the evening went to the mentally handicapped.

We had a lovely room in Lincoln overlooking the cathedral which is floodlit at night – a very beautiful sight. The only trouble was people kept climbing the fire escape next to our room to take pictures of it. The first morning there I woke up in alarm, convinced a crowd of people had come into the room. Fortunately the room was empty, but when I drew back the curtain I hastily let it fall again. Some particularly enterprising tourists had climbed over the fire escape onto the flat roof outside our window and were clicking away at the cathedral from there! I had to creep about with the curtains closed until they'd gone!

After all the kerfufle with tickets and coaches and change of venue I was a bit apprehensive about the evening but the spirit world didn't let me down. When you're worried about something they always come up trumps. In the bathroom – where I always go for a bit of privacy! – I heard the name Maisie Bolton from The Pastures, Barrowby. It was Maisie's Mum.

'I was a medium like you, Doris,' she said. 'My guide was called Topsy.' She wanted to wish her daughter happy birthday she said, because it was her birthday the following week.

Well when I got on stage and tried to find Maisie Bolton from The Pastures, Barrowby, I discovered her Mum had miscalculated Maisie – or Mavis as her name turned out to be, I'd misheard – wasn't there. She'd fallen ill and given the tickets to a close friend.

Her mother was quite put out. She told me her name was Doris like mine and she folded her arms and settled down for a good chat and wouldn't let anyone else in for some time. In the end she agreed to let other spirit people have a turn on condition that Mavis' friend took some flowers to her for her birthday.

'And tell her it's true what I used to say about the after life,' she added as a parting shot, 'I'm here now and it's just as I said.'

Once Doris cleared the line they all came through; a husband who'd left a trilby hat in the wardrobe and was complaining because he'd splashed out on a new suit just before he passed, the mother who knew that her daughter had got a new car and £250 knocked off the price and who worried about her grandson, a lovely boy who 'wouldn't apply himself', a young girl who passed with leukaemia and knew that her sister was wearing her favourite blue sweater but hadn't managed to get into her shoes because they were too small, a mother who complained her family had put artificial flowers beside her picture instead of fresh ones, a little boy who'd left behind £4.75 in his building society account and so it went on . . .

At one point I got a contact for the Richardson family. They were all sitting there in a row, about twelve of them, and I got practically all their names; Donna, Diana, Deborah, Peggy, Alan . . .

It was marvellous. A wonderful evening for me and for the mentally handicapped.

The next day we set off for Bridlington where we were doing two shows and a very lively time we had!

The weather had changed at last and we glided through the Lincolnshire countryside, bathed in warm sunshine. I'd forgotten how pretty Lincolnshire can be. We passed whole fields of shining gold which I took to be mustard, but later Tony Ortzen who was introducing me on stage said, 'Did you see all those fields of rape?'

'Of what?' I asked, horrified.

'Rape,' he grinned, 'that's what it's called.'

'Well we always called it mustard,' I told him, 'I think that's much nicer.'

And as we skimmed through the country lanes I suddenly saw a name that sent the years rolling back. Scampton. My very first station when I was in the WAAFs.

'Oh Robbie, slow down a minute,' I said to the driver. 'There's my old station. I wonder whether they'd let us have a look round and drive down to dispersal.'

This was the place where one cold dawn long ago I'd heard a young airman whistling *The Lord's My Shepherd* as he climbed into his plane and I'd known with absolute certainty that he wasn't coming back. Yes Scampton was the place where I'd come to terms with my psychic power for the first time. It made my heart beat faster just to look at it.

It had been modernized, of course, but the old married quarters where we'd been billeted were still there. We slept under canvas in those days but we used to go to the married quarters to get undressed and get ready to go out and to wait for the buses that took us to our tents for the night.

Robbie stopped the car. 'I'll go and ask them if we can look round,' he said and strode away to the guardroom but sadly it wasn't to be. Apparently you had to write in and make an appointment. I often wonder if I'd thought to ask myself whether it would have made any difference. After all having been in the forces myself I know how to put the question and

207

who to ask for. But there you are I didn't think of it at the time and when I did it was too late.

Disappointed we continued on our way, but the magnificent Humber bridge almost made up for it. It was such a wonderful sight, rolling out and out across the brown water. An incredible feat of engineering.

At our seafront hotel in Bridlington, the lady on the desk was thrown into confusion by our arrival.

'What terms do you want?' she asked.

'Terms?' said Laurie. 'What do you mean?'

'Well, do you want dinner or just bed and breakfast?'

'Oh I don't think we'll want dinner tomorrow night,' I explained. 'We'll be at the theatre, but tonight . . .'

'Surely Doris Stokes can order what she wants,' Laurie interrupted.

'Oh, well, yes – if you like,' but the lady looked a little crestfallen as if she'd much prefer to get things straight in advance.

We were in the area of the great trenchermen of course and when they served you a meal, boy, they served you a meal. No wonder food is the first thing they ask you about.

Oddly enough though, we didn't even see a Yorkshire pudding, not that I'm allowed to eat them these days. But when I was a girl, Yorkshire pudding was a great filler up. We had Yorkshire pudding and gravy before the main course on a Sunday. Then a tiny scrap of meat surrounded by a mound of vegetables and finally to finish, Yorkshire pudding again with jam or sugar and vinegar. It was a good filling meal and I expect the older people still eat it like that.

We phoned the theatre soon after we arrived just to check the arrangements and found the manageress highly perplexed.

'We've had a call from two vicars,' she said. 'They asked if we wanted them to come into the theatre in case anything untoward happened. I didn't know

208

what to say. What do you think? Do you normally have vicars there?'

'No, love, not unless they've bought tickets,' I said, 'but don't worry. Give me the phone numbers and I'll sort it out.'

Well the first vicar was on holiday, so he couldn't have been too worried but the second vicar was at home.

'Hello,' I said, 'it's Doris Stokes here. I understand you've volunteered to come to the theatre. Do you mean you want to come on stage with me?'

'Oh no,' he said, 'I meant did they want me to come and clear out the evil influences afterwards.'

'Evil influences!' I echoed. 'What on earth are you talking about?'

'Well, sometimes, it's happened when we've had people like you here before, it leaves evil influences in the place and we have to go in and clear them out.'

'I can assure you there'll be nothing like that with me,' I said firmly. 'But if you are really so concerned why don't you come on stage with me and warn the people and let them make up their own minds.'

Well he didn't fancy that either but it turned into quite a discussion. He quoted the Bible at me and I quoted the Bible at him, but we weren't really getting anywhere.

'Look,' I said at last, 'I'll tell you what I'll do. I'll give your name and telephone number out so that if anybody is in trouble after seeing me, they can ring you for help.'

There was a small pause. 'Oh, eh – I don't think that would be a very good idea,' said the vicar.

'No? Well that's what you're talking about isn't it? Or do you just want the glory of going into the theatre and doing the whole blessing bit? I thought you were concerned about the people.'

'I am.'

'Well I'll give them your number then,' I said. And I did as well.

But I felt a bit sad as I put the phone down. Why they feel it's wrong to bring joy and strength and comfort to people I don't know. After some demonstrations the love in the air is so thick you can almost see it. How can that possibly be evil?

There wasn't time to dwell on it though because we'd promised to do an interview for Radio Humberside. I'd hesitated at first because I was afraid it might be a long distance to travel, but no they said, they had a studio in Bridlington, we could do it from there.

Well it turned out to be the funniest broadcast I've ever done. The address we'd been given was on the seafront and we pulled up at a strange little building like a cross between a broken down café and a nissan hut. Next door was a funfair and right beside the building a giant swing boat lunged backwards and forwards full of wildly screaming people.

'This can't be right,' said Laurie surveying the place in amazement.

'Well I'm sure this is where they told us to come.' There was a girl at a little tourist information kiosk outside so I asked her.

'Oh yes,' she said, 'there's a studio here. You can go through. I'll give you the key.'

'The key?' I queried my voice going into a squeak. 'Isn't there anyone there?'

'No,' said the girl.

Well we couldn't believe our eyes. We opened the door on a do it yourself studio. It really was radio by numbers. There was a list of instructions: One. Sit comfortably. Two. Pick up the telephone. Three. Dial this number . . . Four. Place yourself in front of the microphone . . .

We were in hysterics. Almost crying with laughter I dialled the number and a young girl answered.

'Oh hello, Doris,' she said. 'The power's by the door. Right, now press that button. Put on the headphones . . .' and so it went on.

The place was double-glazed and absolutely swel-

210

tering that day so we propped the door open with a bucket to get a little air and somehow through our giggles we started the broadcast. Half-way through there was a great clatter. A girl outside had kicked the bucket away.

'Sorry!' she called, 'but we want to use the phone in the other room and we aren't allowed to when this door's open.'

Laurie almost fell off his chair. 'I don't believe this,' he gasped. 'It's *Candid Camera* isn't it? It's not real!'

And over the top of it all, even with the door closed, came the screams from the swing boat.

I don't know what the programme was like but all I can say is I've not had such a good laugh for ages!

On a sadder note it was while we were in Bridlington that the news came of Roy Plomley's passing. We were getting ready to go to the theatre and the television was playing away in the next room, when suddenly I recognized Roy Plomley's voice.

'Roy Plomley's on the television,' I called to John and drifted out of the bathroom to watch. But it was only a recording and afterwards they announced that Roy had passed that morning.

I was very sad because he is such a gentle, loving man. A real old world gentleman. When they showed the list of stars who had been on *Desert Island Discs* I felt very humble and very proud to have been invited. In fact I was one of the last guests on the show. Roy will be sadly missed, not only by his family but by his millions of listeners and by his colleagues at the BBC. He knows now that what I was talking about was true and I hope he has a happy life on the other side. Well I know he will because he was always such a considerate, lovely man.

There was more fun and games when we got to the theatre that night. The dressing-rooms and everything else backstage seemed to be in the basement and when you opened the door from the street, instead of walking forward you went straight down, down these narrow winding stone steps without a handrail. Frightened the life out of me, of course, and I was sure I'd break my neck but I managed it.

Talk about Casey's Court. When it was time to go on stage, there was me holding my long dress up at the front and John holding it up at the back, struggling one in front of the other up these steep steps like some kind of broken down pantomime horse! And when I got on stage and sat down, I nearly shot into the audience! Laurie is a stickler for cleanliness and he'd given the leather seat that had been put out for me, an extra good polish. It looked lovely but it was as slippery as glass and I had to spend the whole evening with my feet braced hard against the floor to stop myself sliding out onto my bum into the auditorium!

Both Bridlington shows were a success thank goodness. I've already mentioned in an earlier chapter Paul Hewson who came to talk to me in my hotel room, but there were many other good contacts. There was a husband who mentioned the £79 his wife had won at bingo. There was ten-year-old Susie who'd been killed in a road accident. 'It was 4.30 and I'd been running, then bang . . . It wasn't fair. I'd only just been to the dentist and I hate the dentist's. I needn't have bothered . . .' There was also a puzzling message about something being rolled up in the toe of a sock.

'Did you find some money in the toe of a sock, or did she use to hide money in a sock. It's something to do with a sock,' I explained.

'I know what that means,' said the young woman at the microphone. 'When I was little we were very very poor and I was hoping for something for Christmas. They got an old sock, filled it with bits of screwed up paper and old hair brushes and things for a joke!'

I also met up with two previous sitters, only one of them was now talking to me from the other side.

'It's Barry,' said a man's voice, 'and I know you.'

I realized then that he must have been for a sitting

but I meet so many people I didn't recognize his voice. Barry said he was with Amanda and looking for Margaret. Well when Margaret came to the front I recognized her face. Hers was one of the *Forty Minutes* sittings that didn't ever reach the screen. She'd come with her husband Barry hoping to contact her daughter Mandy who was in the spirit world. But now it seemed as if fresh tragedy had struck, because Barry was also in the spirit world.

'Oh no, he took himself over, darling,' I said in horror. 'He just wants to say he's sorry. I'd upset her two days before and she sulked a bit,' he said, 'but that wasn't it.' And he went on to explain that he was afraid of being made redundant. 'I was redundant once before then I got another job and I thought I was about to lose that as well. I hadn't got the guts to face it . . .'

Most of all he wanted his wife to know that it wasn't anything she'd done, and he still loved her.

During question time a dear little lad came up. He was only two pennyworth and he looked up at me on the stage and said I've read your books and I would like to ask is there room for everyone up there or do we move on?

Well I explained that it takes hundreds of years to move on and there seems to be room for all and he trotted back to his seat, but at the end of the show he came back again with his book to sign and they hoisted him up onto the stage so that I could give him a big hug.

That night they gave me a standing ovation and through the cheers and shouts I detected a familiar chant: 'Doris Stokes . . . Doris Stokes . . .' I looked up at the balcony and there was the girl who'd shown John the cardboard cut-out she'd pinched from the book signing all those months ago. She'd come with a great bunch of friends plus the cut-out and they stood there waving it above their heads as they chanted. Gradually the rest of the audience took up the chant until the whole theatre was swaying to the rhythm of 'Doris Stokes! Doris Stokes!'

It was the most magical moment.

As it turned out I was to have a more lasting reminder of Bridlington and that wonderful evening than my own memories. When I got home there was a letter waiting for me from Kathy Nicholson who'd been in the audience:

> Dear Doris, I just felt that I wanted to write to you to say thank you from the bottom of my heart for bringing my little boy Steven to talk to me last night. Everything you said about his accident and how he was put onto a machine to help his breathing, and the fact that he would have been a cabbage if he'd lived, were all so very accurate. His personality came through so very real and I feel so much love towards you because of what you did for me. I would just like to say Doris that right at the beginning of the demonstration you gave us a 'Mrs Roberts' then at one point you said 'Kathy' or 'Katharine' and then later you said 'Caravan' but then you said 'Oh I don't know what all that is about' and there was a group of ladies gathered at the front acknowledging your messages.
>
> I didn't stand up at the time because I was a little confused but I firmly believe now Doris that my Dad, Arthur Roberts, was trying to talk to me. He passed over almost 18 months ago and I have always looked for comfort in the belief that Steven and his Grandad were together in the spirit world because they were very close.
>
> My name is Kathy and at the moment we live in a caravan until we move into our new home. I would be very pleased if you would accept a little gift from me. The cassette enclosed is one I recorded last year. You see I play the trumpet and my Dad was very proud of me and I dedicated

my cassette to him. He never got to hear it whilst on the earth plane and I *know* now that he knows all about my recording the cassette and also that he and Steven enjoy listening to it in the spirit world.

God bless you, Doris.

My sincerest best wishes to you and to your dear husband, John,

Yours sincerely
Kathy Nicholson (née Roberts)

Well I played that cassette and it's absolutely beautiful. Kathy is a very talented girl and her music has given me great pleasure. What's more, when I close my eyes and listen to *Danny Boy*, and all the other old favourites, I'm back on that stage in Bridlington surrounded by a great wall of love.

Readers who've got this far will realize that all kinds of wonderful things have happened since my last book! The most exciting of all, however, was being presented to Princess Anne, when she opened the new Bone Marrow Unit at Westminster Hospital.

As I mentioned in a *Host of Voices*, *Woman's Own* magazine launched an appeal to build the unit as part of their support for the Save the Children Fund. Well they raised over a million pounds I believe, and I was able to contribute £12,000 from my own charity shows which was marvellous. The unit was built and on June 6th it was opened by Princess Anne who is president of the Save the Children Fund.

Naturally I'd been looking forward to the ceremony for months and months. I'd got my clothes sorted out. I was going to wear a mandarin style dress in spiritual colours of swirling blues and mauves.

Then just the day before the ceremony I had a slight stroke. I was horrified, not so much by my physical condition as the fact that I might miss the presentation and also two appearances I was supposed to be doing in Brighton immediately afterwards. My right arm was clumsy and almost useless and when I tried to speak it came out as a terrible stammer.

'There is no way you can stand up on a stage and talk to people,' said my wonderful doctor when I finally stuttered out what was worrying me. 'You are not to do any work whatsoever. But I don't see why you shouldn't go to the presentation. It'll do you good because you'll enjoy it and you won't have to do any work. Afterwards, though, I want you in hospital for a check-up.'

Sadly, I had to cancel my Brighton appearances but I did struggle along to Westminster Hospital and I'm so glad that I did.

They looked after me marvellously. Professor Hobbs met me at the door and arranged for a nurse to be with me throughout. Then they took me into the boardroom and let me sit there in a chair intended for a lady-in-waiting, until Princess Anne arrived.

She looked breathtaking. I don't know how to describe her; chic, elegant, immaculate – nothing quite captures the way she looked. She was wearing a cream skirt with a navy blue jacket and her hair was swept up and topped by a cream hat with navy blue spots.

She really is a lovely girl. Very slim and upright with a serious expression until she smiles, and then it's like magic. Her whole face lights up with such radiance that you can see how beautiful she really is.

I was last in line to be presented. In front of me were other fund raisers; Miss Jackie Berger, Pauline and Brendan McAleese from Northern Ireland and then me.

I was terrified I might fall over or do something stupid before she got to me, and as she moved along the line my heart was crashing in my ears so loud I thought everyone in the room must be able to hear it. And then, there she was.

'May I present Doris Fisher Stokes, ma'am, who is a medium, writes books and who has worked unstint-

ingly for the Save the Children Fund,' said Iris Burton
editor of *Woman's Own*, while I tried to do a little bob.

The Princess looked directly into my eyes so that
the rest of the room disappeared.

'Have you lost any children with this?' she asked,
referring to the blood diseases that would be treated.

'No, ma'am,' I said, 'I lost four children when I was
young but I just love kids, so I try to do what I can.'

She smiled, 'You look a little bit tired.'

She was observant too. 'Well I don't work as hard
as you, ma'am.'

'Oh it's a little bit different for me!' she said giving
a lopsided grin as if to say it's all laid on for me. I
don't have to work like you do.

And then it was over and she was moving towards
the platform for the speeches. I think perhaps I didn't
pay quite as much attention to the speeches as I
should, because we were standing the whole time.
The chairman offered Princess Anne a chair but she
said, 'No I will stand,' and so everyone else had to
stand up too.

It seemed endless. I braced my back against the wall
and I didn't know whether to stand with my legs
pressed together or apart to balance myself. It went
on and on and the room grew very hot yet Princess
Anne never moved once. Everyone else got a bit
fidgety and even the man on the platform was fanning
himself discreetly with his programme behind the
Princess's back. Princess Anne, however, didn't move
a muscle, she didn't perspire. She simply stood
relaxed, attentive and as cool as if there was a pleasant
breeze blowing.

I looked at her and I thought, my God, that's
breeding, that's royal training for you. You can't buy
what that girl's got.

The ceremony moved on. The Princess unveiled a
blue and gold commemorative plaque and she was
presented with a bouquet of flowers and a plate by a
little girl and a little boy.

The boy turned out to be Mark, the first boy to have had a successful bone marrow transplant. He'd been at the Dorchester when we launched the appeal and he remembered me. Down came the blue rope that separated us and he came over to give me a hug.

'Did I do it right?' he asked. He'd been told to bow and he'd given a quick duck of his head.

'You did it beautifully,' I told him.

Afterwards we went off for a buffet tea and dear Professor Hobbs had arranged for a table to be carried in for me with my own waiter and waitress to bring me the goodies so that I wouldn't have to stand in the queue.

Mr and Mrs McAleese from Northern Ireland were at my table and I thought they were a wonderful couple. They'd lost their little boy before the unit was built but they'd gone ahead to help raise money so that other children could be saved. And they'd managed it all despite the fact that Brendan was unemployed.

I wasn't supposed to be working of course but while we were chatting I suddenly heard the name David and a little boy's voice said something about his sister.

I didn't want to jump in until I was sure so I asked Pauline innocently if she had any other children.

'Oh, yes, a little girl,' she said.

That was it, I must be talking to her son.

'Who's David?' I asked.

'Why that's my little boy's name!' she said.

'He tells me you got a red sweater out of his drawer the other day and buried your face in it.'

She looked stunned. 'Yes I did, two days ago. But nobody knows about that. I didn't even tell Brendan.'

'Well David was with you love,' I said.

I had to be careful not to go into a sitting of course but I was able to give her a few more words of comfort including the fact that David knew his sister was staying with her Auntie Marie while her parents were in London.

Strangely enough we were joined by a very nice young man who'd raised a lot of money in Germany. His name was Flight Leutenant John Foster who worked for the Ministry of Defence. When I told him about my visit to Scampton he said what a pity it was that he hadn't met me then.

'I could have got you in,' he said. 'Just let me know if there's anywhere you'd like to go and I'll arrange it,' and he left me his telephone number.

They were a cheeky lot on our table. They wanted to smoke so they shouted, 'Doris Stokes wants to smoke!' And immediately an ashtray was brought.

Then a bit later somebody wanted to go to the loo. They went out and found they weren't allowed through because Princess Anne was coming down the stairs. So back they came and said: 'Doris Stokes wants to go to the ladies' room!'

'That'll be all right,' they said.

Of course I had to go then but this blonde lady tucked on behind me.

'What did you do that for?' I asked her, 'I could have waited.'

'Well I wanted to go, too,' she said, 'but nobody knows me. Everybody knows you!'

After tea Professor Hobbs came to take me up to see the unit. I'd read in my programme that the unit contained seven special cubicles, five of which are laminar flow cubicles, each with its own filter system bathing the patient with germ free air. There was also a sterile kitchen and utility room.

It sounded very impressive but it was even more impressive when you saw it. There were all these filters and big germ free bubbles.

'Put your hand just there, Doris,' said Professor Hobbs and when I did as he asked I felt a great rush of sterile air pushing against my hand.

There was one little boy in the unit who had already had his transplant and didn't need to be kept in isolation.

219

'This is Matthew,' said Professor Hobbs.

'Hello, Matthew darling,' I said. He was a dear little boy of about three who was lying on his bed with his head on his Daddy's knees. His hair was just beginning to grow back like a little haze of fur all over his head.

'Tummy's going down now isn't it Matthew,' said Professor Hobbs. 'He had a big tummy a little while ago.'

'Aren't you lucky,' I said, 'I've got a big tummy and mine's not going to go down!'

There was a photographer hovering about and he asked if I could get on the bed with Matthew for the picture.

'Yes that's all right,' said Professor Hobbs.

'Can I sit on the bed with you, Matthew?' I asked.

'Yeth.'

'Can I give you a big hug?'

'Yeth,' he said again, so, of course, I did.

It only remained for me to present the doll from Cornwall, now named Anne and resplendent in a red velvet dress and bonnet with underclothes and panties and shoes and socks that all came off and then it was time to go.

I suddenly realized I was exhausted but I wouldn't have missed it for the world.

So here I am in my hospital bed, a bit battered and bruised and playing Kathy's tape to cheer myself up. The doctors shake their heads and tell me I should slow down but I'm busy doing my arm exercises and singing away to get my voice back. I'm determined to be on my feet again soon.

I'm not getting any younger, of course, and I don't know how much longer I've got, none of us does, but I've got a strange feeling that there's still something else I have to do. I can't think what it can be because I've done private sittings, public demonstrations, television, radio and newspaper interviews. Yet I still feel there's something I must do.

No doubt the spirit world will show me what it is in their own good time – and when I find out – you'll be the first to know!